Mary Elizabeth Herbert

Love

Or Self-sacrifice: a story

Mary Elizabeth Herbert

Love
Or Self-sacrifice: a story

ISBN/EAN: 9783741192852

Manufactured in Europe, USA, Canada, Australia, Japa

Cover: Foto ©Andreas Hilbeck / pixelio.de

Manufactured and distributed by brebook publishing software (www.brebook.com)

Mary Elizabeth Herbert

Love

SELF-SACRIFICE.

LONDON: PRINTED BY
SPOTTISWOODE AND CO., NEW-STREET SQUARE
AND PARLIAMENT STREET

LOVE

OR

SELF-SACRIFICE.

A Story.

BY

LADY HERBERT.

LONDON:
RICHARD BENTLEY, NEW BURLINGTON STREET,
PUBLISHER IN ORDINARY TO HER MAJESTY.
1868.

TO

MY BROTHER,

WHO FIRST MADE ME FULLY UNDERSTAND

BY HIS LIFE

THE FULL MEANING AND BEAUTY OF SELF-SACRIFICE,

𝕿𝖍𝖎𝖘 𝕷𝖎𝖙𝖙𝖑𝖊 𝕿𝖆𝖑𝖊

IS

AFFECTIONATELY DEDICATED.

PREFACE.

THIS simple tale is in the main true. I have altered dates and names, but the leading facts remain, though the actors are long since dead.

Had I created an imaginary heroine, I should not have made her contract a marriage utterly unjustifiable on principle, from any mistaken view of duty and self-sacrifice. Neither could I have imagined her binding herself by promise to a man without honour and without faith, and thereby bartering the soul of her child for a possible worldly advantage.

But I have painted Gwladys as she was, as I myself knew her, with all her charms and all her faults.

I have done so to show the life-long suffering we may entail on ourselves by acting on even a generous impulse, without considering that there are lines of right and wrong clearly laid down for each one of us, and from which no consideration should induce us to depart.

And her story may lead my readers to feel as I have done in writing it: how tenderly our Heavenly Father deals with us His creatures, overruling sometimes even our grievous faults for our eventual good, mercifully accepting whatever is honest in our desires to do right, and restoring to us even earthly blessings after a season of sorrow, repentance, and probation.

MARY ELIZABETH HERBERT.

LOVE; OR, SELF-SACRIFICE.

CHAPTER I.

'The Rights of Women.' What are they?
The right to labour and to pray;
The right to comfort in distress;
The right, when others curse, to bless;
The right to love whom others scorn;
The right to comfort all who mourn.
Such 'Woman's Rights!' Such God will bless,
And grant support or give success.

IT was a lovely evening in the Mauritius in April 18—. The setting sun was sinking behind a grove of palms with an underwood of bananas, lighting up their foliage with those wonderful tints which painters of southern skies so well know, and throwing flickering shadows across a path shaded by an avenue of cinnamon trees, of which the small flowering clusters sent forth a fragrant and aromatic smell. Different varieties of large convolvulus, bright blue and pale buff, hung in graceful festoons from bush to bush; while an extensive coffee plantation, with its red berries and star-like white flowers, crept up the side of the hill above the house. No sound was heard but that of the 'Calfat,' a little bird, in size between a sparrow and a linnet, with rose-coloured breast and bill, so called from the noise it makes in the woods when striking the trees with its bill in search of insects; and at the foot of a fine cabbage-palm, a paradise 'Grakle' was sitting on her nest, undisturbed by the vicinity of the inhabitants of the cottage, who treated her as a pet, and from whom she had learnt a variety of phrases with even greater accuracy than the parrot tribe.

Resting on a low divan in the verandah of a picturesque dwelling, one story high, from which the too powerful rays of the tropical sun had been carefully shaded by bamboo blinds, sat a young girl of seventeen, in deep and earnest thought. At first sight she would have scarcely been called beautiful; her complexion was dark and inclined to be sallow, and her features wanted the regularity of perfect beauty. But to those who knew her, these faults were forgotten in the effect produced by her eyes, large, lustrous, speaking, with a whole world in them of passion and of power, and yet melting into wonderful tenderness at the least touch of sorrow, or at the first sight of pain. A profusion of dark hair, banded smoothly near her face, and wound in a cable round her head, gave a slight increase to a height which was a little above the ordinary size. Her figure, slight and girlish, was concealed by the folds of a white muslin dress, confined at the waist by a blue sash; while a veil of the same thrown partly back off her face gave a kind of aureola to her beauty, of which intense purity was the striking characteristic. She had been arranging flowers in a large vase on the table before her, twining a branch of the lovely turquoise blue ipomea round the stem, so as to make a contrast with the delicate ferns, the scarlet poncettia, and the sweet jessamine above. A taller glass was already filled with the large white datura and brilliant scarlet hybiscus; for Gwladys had a passion for flowers, and wonderful taste in their arrangement and in the combination of colours. But to-day she had paused in her occupation, and was listlessly holding a branch of the fan-palm in her hand to brush off the flies, when some one came behind her through the ever-open door, and a kind and fatherly voice said:

'Well, Gwladys, my child, dreaming, as usual, over your flowers? When will the chapel be ready for to-morrow's feast, I wonder?'

The speaker was a man of venerable aspect, in the dress of a French abbé. His form was spare and attenuated; but a look of wonderful charity and benevolence lit up a face which once had laid claim to no small share of masculine beauty.

'O dear Père Marquet, is it you?' exclaimed Gwladys, springing from her seat and joyfully kissing his hand. 'You must not scold me for dreaming, for I was only thinking of what you said last week on the way God gives us flowers, beautiful things, little 'way-side' pleasures all day long, to cheer us on our way, and make us praise Him and love Him more and more. I shouldn't like to be a Sister of Charity for that one thing only, that I might not smell these delicious roses!' plunging her nose as she spoke into a bunch in the vase beside her. 'But now,' she continued, gaily, 'you are going to stay with me, are you not? —at least, for to-night? Annette will be out of her wits with joy at having to get your room ready.'

'Yes, my child,' replied the Père Marquet, 'I will stay. I want to know how you are getting on with your school, and half a dozen other things. And your father?'

A sudden cloud came over the young girl's face. She looked down, and said, timidly, 'He is not at home. I believe he is gone on board one of the English ships with Lord William de Tracey, a young man whom he brought here last week, and whom he has taken a great fancy to. But I *hate* him!' she added, the colour mounting up to her brow as she said the words; and then, passing out of the verandah into the house, went to give directions for the comfort of her guest.

The old priest sighed sadly as she closed the door behind her. Full well he knew the difficult path that poor child had to tread. Left motherless at her birth, and an only child, it had devolved on an old and faithful nurse to care for the little life which had already cost so much. Mrs. Murray had been married but one short year and in that time had learned all the misery which can be borne by a woman who finds herself wedded to one without heart and without faith, who had married her for her money and for her beauty, and nought besides; and who had added to her bitterness by cruelty and neglect, and an open preference for another when his momentary passion for her had passed. But, sad and mournful as her married life had been, her very sorrows had matured her for the great change. Aided by the fatherly advice and unwearied patience of the Père Marquet, she had learned to understand in its fulness the meaning of that cross which God had given her to bear. And so she had bowed her head meekly under it and accepted it from His hand, and learned what the love was which passeth knowledge, and which was leading her surely and safely to her rest. The night before her confinement she had a long and earnest talk with her maid—a French Catholic—who had lived with her during her happy girlhood, which had known no cloud, and who had accompanied her when she exchanged a father's love and tenderness for the passionate, fitful temper of a man whom she soon found it was as impossible to love as to respect. To this faithful servant she entrusted her coming child, with a presentiment, too truly to be realised, that she should not survive her time of trial.

'You know my mind, Annette,' were her concluding words, 'and I feel sure you will carry out my wishes.' These were her last words of earthly caring. The Père Marquet had stayed with her to the last, and prepared her soul for the struggle with wise and loving ministrations. She received the last sacraments with perfect consciousness and fervent acts of faith and contrition, and then the end came; and a frail baby flower was all that was left to tell of suffering over and victory won.

No wonder that the kind and tender old man felt drawn to that weeping nurse and that desolate child! And when, half an hour after, Colonel Murray came in, scarcely sober, and with a half-repentant, half-defiant manner looked on the face of his dead wife, and then coldly and carelessly on the pledge of love she had left him in the cradle by her side, both pity and anger were kindled in the priest's heart, and he registered a vow that henceforth that little child's soul should be his special care and thought. And so the little Gwladys grew up, carefully nursed and tended physically by the faithful Annette, and equally cared for morally and spiritually by him who had given that promise by her mother's deathbed. Her father was simply indifferent to her for the first few years. Then, as her prettiness began to dawn upon him, he would, from time to time, show her some marks of kindness and favour. But, on the whole, Gwladys feared more than she loved him; and when she grew older and he began to insist on her appearing at dinner and doing the honours of his house to his guests, who were mostly of a 'fast' and rollicking description, her shrinking aversion to the whole thing increased. Her greatest pleasure was in sitting on a low stool at Père Marquet's feet on the occasion of his frequent visits, listening to his gentle instructions, or to the oft-repeated tale of her mother's childhood and early death. He directed her studies likewise, and employed her in visiting the sick and suffering among the poor negroes, squatted here and there between the neighbouring plantations, who all knew and loved her, and among whom her quick step and sunny smile were ever hailed as the harbingers of charity and kindness. For Gwladys could not understand the prejudice existing in some minds against the coloured races; it was the greatest pleasure to her to find herself at church kneeling by their side, or to receive holy water from their hand, and lately, with the consent of the Père Marquet, she had opened a little school of black and coolie children, whom she taught herself, and found wonderfully quick and ready at receiving instruction. Her childhood, on the whole, may be said to have been happy, though rather solitary, and her girlhood still more so, until an event occurred which coloured her whole future life.

Among the rare and somewhat distant neighbours whom Colonel Murray's exceptional conduct had not entirely estranged from occasional visits to the cottage, was a widow lady, a Mrs. Vere, who, with three children, lived in a plantation on the opposite side of the island. She had known and loved Gwladys' mother, who had been her schoolfellow and companion as a girl, and felt the tenderest compassion and sympathy for the worse than orphan child. Now and then Colonel Murray would give leave to Gwladys to spend a few days with this old friend, a permission which filled Gwladys with delight, and which was reckoned among the rare treats of her otherwise commonplace and colourless existence. The charm and tenderness of Mrs. Vere's manner, her gentle gaiety, softened only by the ever-living remembrance of her great sorrow, and, above all, her warm, eager, and enthusiastic piety, gave her a singular hold on Gwladys' heart and mind. When the day was fixed for one of these promised visits, she would listen for hours to catch the first sound of Mrs. Vere's carriage-wheels; and when once she found herself side by side with her old friend, and actually on her way to the 'Wilderness,' as Mrs. Vere's home was called, her joy knew no bounds. And the whole tone of the house was one in all ways helpful to the formation of Gwladys' character. Captain Vere had inherited this property about twenty-six years before, and set himself immediately to work to raise and improve the condition of the negro population around him. And this was no easy task. Emancipation had taken place, but no corresponding attempts had been made to educate the race so freed, who found themselves suddenly thrown on their own resources, without either the knowledge or the habits which would enable them to lead a life of honest independence. Taught all their lives that labour was a curse, and unaccustomed to self-reliance of any sort, they lived miserably on the fruits of the soil in the woods or in the purlieus of Port Louis: while the planters, finding it was impossible to rely upon them for getting in their crops, and that they preferred starving to working, imported their labourers from Hindostan, upwards of 200,000 of whom were soon settled in the colony. These coolies were hired, as in the West Indies, under five years' engagements, their rights being protected by the stipendiary magistrates; at the end of that time they might, if they wished, return to their own country, and were sent back free of expense. The negroes, by degrees, formed themselves into little communities, cultivating small patches of ground for their own support, and occasionally doing odd jobs for such of the planters as acted kindly towards them. They lived, however, in great poverty; while religiously, they were even in a worse state. From the paucity of clergy, they had been left, comparatively, without any Christian instruction, and Captain Vere and his young wife almost began to despair at the magnitude of the task which their consciences had moved them to undertake. But they had in themselves the elements of success, which consisted not only in a tender charity and patience which no indifference or ingratitude could discourage, but likewise in an earnest faith and persevering energy which would yield before no obstacle to attain their end.

When Captain Vere brought his fair young bride to their new home, the negro population turned out in great numbers to welcome them, partly from curiosity, but many in consequence of the reputation for kindness and justice which had preceded them.

When, at last, the crowds had dispersed, and they had been left in peace and alone in their new home, Captain Vere, drawing his wife closer to him, said to her gently and tenderly:

'You see all these poor people, my darling!

you will help me, will you not, to spend and be spent for them?'

A closer pressure of the arm he held was the only reply: but the compact thus sealed, nobly did each fulfil.

And so their married life began: in mutual love, and trust, and work, and sacrifice. They had learnt the secret of all earthly happiness, in devotion to others for the love of God. At first, the difficulties seemed almost insurmountable; all the old planters were against them, and treated their proposals as the schemes of young and enthusiastic visionaries, even if no worse.

'Nothing is to be done with these black people,' they would exclaim. 'As for trying to regenerate them, you may as well try to civilise the monkeys themselves. They are as lazy and obstinate as they are ungrateful and vindictive, and they are so hopelessly stupid and demoralised that it is impossible to give them the faintest ideas of religious truth.'

So the changes rang on this ever-fruitful theme; and after some months of patient striving, the Veres began to fear that there was more truth in these allegations than they had at first believed. Still, they were determined to persevere. The bishop of Port Louis, a Benedictine, and a man of singular holiness and goodness, had lately imported into the island a congregation founded by the Abbé Liebermann, whose main object was the conversion of the negro race. The local superior of this religious order was the Abbé Laval, a man remarkable for the austerity of his life, his apostolic zeal, his humility, and his love of the poor. Born in Normandy in 1803, he lost his mother very young, and was sent by his father to Paris to be educated as a doctor. He took his medical degree in 1830, and then returning home, practised in his native place; but being a man of independent fortune, the greater part of his time was spent in field sports, especially in hunting, for which he had a positive passion. A terrible accident, in which his horse was killed by falling down a precipice, and in which he himself escaped as by a miracle, seems to have changed the whole current of his thoughts, and like St. Ignatius, nothing would content him but to devote himself henceforth entirely to the service of God and of His poor. He entered, in consequence, into the Theological College of St. Sulpice, and was ordained priest in 1838. Burning with but one wish, that of devoting himself to some missionary work, he gladly answered the appeal of Bishop Collier to accompany him to the Mauritius for the evangelisation of the negroes. In an account published after his death, it is related that he received the summons in the middle of the night, in the presbytery of his little humble country cure, and making the sign of the cross, started instantly, without taking leave of any one, and with only his breviary under his arm. He arrived in the island on September 14, 1841, and began by learning the dialect of the creoles, a most astonishing French patois, which none but the natives can, at first, understand. This patois, nevertheless, has crystallised into a genuine grammatical language, affording an example of how modern languages have been made. This difficulty was, however, soon overcome by the Père Laval's unwearied zeal and charity; but, at first, as with the Veres, his instructions seemed to fall on hearts of ice. Nothing appeared to soften the hearts or awaken the intelligence of the negro race. The holy priest was pained; but instead of relaxing in his efforts, he only redoubled his prayers, his fasts, and his mortifications. After much patient waiting, and apparently fruitless toil, the good seed at last bore fruit. The evening instructions at the Cathedral of St. Louis became crowded, and the negroes eagerly flocked to the church both before and after their daily labours. Knowing that the old were mainly to be gained through the young, the Abbé Laval collected the children every day for catechetical instruction, and opened schools in every possible direction. And soon the result made itself felt: the children went home and spread the good seed in their respective villages. A little child of ten or twelve years old might be seen, sitting on a stool in the middle of a hut, teaching the catechism to his father and mother, and these listening with docility and even eagerness to his instructions. Little by little, the work grew and prospered: and when once they had been taught, the negro fervour knew no bounds. They would frequently walk to church, a distance of fourteen or fifteen miles, always taking care to arrive long before the service began; and they observed the fast days of the church with a rigour unknown in Europe, tasting nothing till after sunset. The news of this religious movement spread rapidly into the interior of the island, and Captain Vere lost no time in applying for one of these missionaries for his own people. Seconded by the zealous love of his wife, a chapel was built, schools opened, and the whole face of the country changed. The negroes became industrious, quiet, and well-behaved, and their zeal exceeded even that of their instructors. There was one poor woman who lived exactly twenty miles from the nearest church. She used to walk that distance every month, and sometimes oftener, to perform her religious duties. She came on the Saturday, went to confession, and the next day to Holy Communion: and then walked back again. Nor was the length of road the only difficulty she had to surmount. There was a river to cross, of which the bridge had been swept away by a hurricane; and her husband used to accompany her and drag her through the water, which was sometimes up to her waist. He would then leave her to walk the rest of the way in her wet clothes, and the following day meet her again on her return home and drag her again through the river! What could not be done with souls animated by a zeal like this? Captain and Mrs. Vere did indeed see the fruit of their labours; but it was not permitted for him to enjoy it long. An illness, insidious in its nature, but hopeless as to cure, cut short a life so full of usefulness and unselfish charity, and Mrs. Vere was left, with her little children, to face the world alone.

> 'Alone she sat, *alone!* that worn-out word,
> So idly spoken, and so coldly heard;
> Yet all that poets sing and grief hath known
> Of hope laid waste, knells in that word—ALONE!'

There are many forms and degrees of suffering in this life: many agonising moments and heart-breaking hours, when the will strives in vain to acquiesce in the Hand that has stricken the blow, but none are as bad as this. The utter loneliness, the hopeless desolation, the cold dreariness, day and night, from which there is no escape. The waking up from a troubled slumber to find the horrible void, and to feel that it must be for ever, and for ever, and for ever, as long as this weary life lasts, this it is which makes widowhood one of the heaviest crosses which our Heavenly Father can lay upon His children. Then, the having no one like-minded, with whom to share the joys and troubles of daily life; no one to consult with about the children, who has a real understanding of their character and peculiarities; and the additional suffering of kindly-meant but ill-timed or ill-judged words of so-called consolation, and of painful interference in family affairs from relations and friends, with the jealousies and ill-nature and misunderstandings of others. All these things Mrs. Vere felt with a keenness, and at times with a bitterness, which, during the first few months, it seemed impossible for her to control.

To every one, there comes in life, a great turning-point for good or evil, and this is generally brought about by some crushing sorrow. We are put in the crucible, and it depends on the nature of the metal whether it be thereby purified or annihilated. Mrs. Vere passed through her fiery trial outwardly much as others had done before her; but in reality, the whole woman was changed. Her life was over: the life that it was a pleasure to live ; the life which used to send her with a singing gladness in her heart to her daily occupations; the life which had been so brightened by ever-increasing love and sympathy, and by the consciousness of being a real helpmeet to the man she reverenced and idolised—all this was past.

But one thing remained, and that was *duty*.

Duty to him to whom she had vowed her life, and in fulfilling whose lightest behest she felt strength and consolation. For she could not look upon him as dead, but as gone abroad; —as gone before her to their common home, where, in God's own time and way she would join him. When the first overpowering months of agony were passed, therefore, she gathered herself up for the strife of life, and resolved to do battle gallantly; never to shrink or falter in the path which he had marked out for her; to walk on, though, may be, with bleeding feet, on that thorny and unprotected road; in a word, to suffer and be strong.

Her first duty was to her children; to train them as he would have wished, to set before them, through their father's example, the beauty of self-sacrifice, the glory of work— earnest work—that labour which Carlyle so justly calls 'worship,' and which emanates from that double precept of the Gospel law of love to God and man.

Next to her children, were the people dependent on her; the servants around their home, the negroes whom he had reclaimed, the coolies whom he was trying to teach. Had she been free from these obligations and ties, her life would have been far easier. She felt the attraction which all real widows must feel, to a life of charity, penance, and prayer; to a total withdrawal from the world, which had ceased to have any charms for her, and which, on the contrary, could only henceforth be to her a scene of painful and sad memories, calling forth all the endurance, courage, and self-control of her nature. But another path was marked out for her by God's providence, and a far keener martyrdom. She took it in all its length and breadth, and *accepted* it; and having done so, hers was not a nature to look back. With wonderful energy and incessant toil, she set herself to the task of completing all that her husband had begun or contemplated. And the work brought its reward, in taking her so completely out of herself, that she had no time for selfish tears. True, there were evenings, when, wearied with the day's toil, harassed by unexpected opposition where she had the most right to look for support, or worried with the faults and shortcomings of her children, who, as yet, were unable to grasp the high standard she wished to set before them—there were times, I say, when her brave spirit would fail, and her tears would flow, almost in spite of herself, at having no loving encouraging word to cheer her on, no tender smile to greet her coming home, no one to say the 'well done!' which used ever to greet the fulfilment of her daily task. But these moments of depression were rare. She knew where to lay her heavy burden down, and Who alone knew all, and would feel for all.

By degrees, her little Walter—her only boy —began to understand a little more of her life and purpose. His was a noble nature—generous, sensitive, vehement, and loving, with the simplicity and purity of a little child. His love for his mother became the great passion of his life. To give her some little pleasure, to defend her from injury and wrong, to be her protector and her friend—these were the dreams of his chivalrous boyhood. A mixture of both father and mother, he inherited from the former that hatred of a lie, that nobility of purpose, and that contempt for luxury and worldly things, which had made Captain Vere trample on conventional usages, for the sake of solid and permanent results; while from the latter, he had imbibed the enthusiasm, generosity, tenderness, and delicacy of feeling, which threw a halo round her real saintliness, and which he worshipped with all the passionate devotion of which his beautiful nature was capable. Two baby girls completed Mrs. Vere's home circle—twin flowers, born in the midst of ever-increasing anxiety for the health of him who was dearer to her than life; cradled in the midst of the overwhelming sorrow which had crushed her to the earth, they yet, strange to say, were the gayest, gladdest children that could be met with on a summer's day. At first, their merry laugh was almost insupportable to their widowed mother; she would bury her head in her hands, and try to shut it out. But by degrees, she became thankful for her little sunbeams, her 'Mayflowers,' as she called them—thankful that no cloud had dimmed their little bright faces, and that she was thus better able to carry out one of her husband's last instructions to her: 'Do not sadden the home, for the sake of the children.'

Thus tranquilly, if not happily, passed Mrs. Vere's widowhood. She became the providence of the whole country-side. No one was in sorrow, or sickness, or trouble, without coming to or sending for her: her little room was like a confessional, in which every one poured out to her their difficulties or woes; sure of a patient hearing, wise advice, or soothing word, even if not of more substantial consolation. Her soft and sad yet loving face was found by every sick and dying bed; and she learned, by those ever-recurring scenes of suffering and trial, more entirely to forget herself, and what was the true secret of the peace which passeth all understanding.

In this loving and genial atmosphere, Gwladys gladly took refuge from the ambiguous kindness of her father, and the solitariness of her motherless home. Little by little, she became as one of themselves, and on the same footing with Mrs. Vere as her own children. But as, day by day, her character developed itself, and the prettiness of a child merged into the more thoughtful beauty of a woman, a change came over her intercourse with Walter. She avoided being alone with him, would make various little excuses to stay with Mrs. Vere in her cool sitting-room, or to string garlands for the tinies, or to visit the sick at the stations near, who all had learned to know and love her. And yet, when he came in, her colour would rise, and her eye would brighten, and her whole being felt transformed. Walter, on the other hand, was miserable at the change. He loved her passionately, but it had grown upon him unconsciously: he had seen and known her all his life: she had been his only young companion, for his little sisters were too childish to join in his sports, or still less to share in the aspirations after all that was good and great, and beautiful and self-sacrificing, which for ever filled his mind. Gwladys and he would write imaginary plays of heroes and heroines, and act the different parts, for which Walter had inherited a peculiar talent; or else take some favourite historic character, as Roger, the good King of Sicily, or King Louis of France, and embody these conceptions in drawing or in verse. Trained in the same faith, taught by the same wise and holy pastor, in both there was developed a singleness of purpose, a self-denial in little things, an earnestness for the promotion of God's glory, and a devotion of body, soul and spirit, to the care of His suffering poor, at any personal risk or sacrifice, which unconsciously, yet surely, deepened and intensified their childhood's love, and seemed to make it more of heaven than of earth.

Mrs. Vere silently, tenderly, and with motherly prudence, watched the growth of the intimacy between the two children. An eventual union would crown the wish of her heart, and she foresaw no obstacle, save what might possibly arise from the strangeness and uncertainty of temper of Gwladys' father. Still, she hoped and waited patiently; and when she saw the shyness, which, like the gossamer on the gorse in summer-time, veiled the strong and beautiful life of love which was developing itself in Gwladys' heart, she silently rejoiced, only trembling at the knowledge of the pain which she knew her boy must go through before his eyes were opened, and he could realise the inestimable value of the treasure he had won. For women in these matters are developed earlier than men, and a girl passes through a whole world of thought and feeling before a boy of the same age has understood the first letter of that magic word which transforms the whole nature, and gives to life a force and a beauty which was utterly unknown before.

At the time my story opens, Walter was twenty. He had passed successfully through the different courses of study attainable in the island, and it had become a matter of anxious thought with Mrs. Vere, whether she should keep him with her, and initiate him into the business connected with the working of the estate, or send him first for a couple of years to Europe, to complete his education. In appearance, he was tall, dark, and well-formed, with thick clustering brown hair, fine eyes, and a beautiful mouth, the short upper lip quivering at the least emotion of pleasure or pain. The twins, Margaret and Maude, were fair and blue eyed, and so much alike, that strangers were perpetually taking one for the other, to the great amusement of the children themselves, who resorted to endless little playful devices to increase their friends' perplexity.

During one of these rare and pleasant episodes in Gwladys' life, an expedition had been planned by Mrs. Vere, to go, by part of the primeval forest, to a picturesque bay a few miles lower down the coast. Home worries had told on Gwladys' sensitive temperament, and Mrs. Vere thought that a more complete distraction than was afforded by their ordinary quiet home life, would cheer and do her good. So the day was fixed, the ponies ordered, provisions sent on beforehand, and, in spite of some rather ominous lowering clouds, and a heavy sultry feeling which betokened an impending storm, the merry party started in high spirits for their pic-nic. Hardly had they reached, however, the outskirts of the forest, through the borders of which their path lay, than one of the twins, little Maude, became sick and faint; the oppressive heat and steamy sultriness of the wood, into which no sea-breeze could penetrate, had been too much for a frame naturally frail and delicate; so Mrs. Vere resolved to take her quietly home, leaving the rest with her governess, Madame Latour, a gentle, pleasing, lady-like woman, to act as chaperone, and take her place in the expedition. The destined spot was reached, after a steep scramble up the thickly-wooded hill, from the top of which they were rewarded by a lovely view of the blue sea and sandy bays beneath their feet, to which they descended through a tangled mass of glorious tropical vegetation, Gwladys feeling a strong inclination every moment to stop her pony, and gather some of the beautiful ferns and orchids which he was ruthlessly trampling under his feet. Once safely landed in the little bay, the party, whose pleasure had been somewhat damped by Maude's illness and Mrs. Vere's absence, began to recover their spirits, and after luncheon, Walter proposed to Gwladys to go to a little village near the shore, which formed, as it were, the centre of a semicircle of hills whose precipitous sides descended to the sea. Leaving little Margaret to collect shells and coral with Madame Latour on the sea-shore, they toiled up the steep ascent, and had nearly reached the summit, when the storm, without any previous warning, burst upon them with a fury which threatened instant destruction. The rain, falling like a deluge on the red hill sides, stripped them bare of both soil and crops; a tiny river was changed, as in a moment, into a mighty torrent, and came dashing down to the ocean, carrying with it masses of timber, rock and stone, whilst the resistless impetuosity of the wind, which had risen to a hurricane, and seemed to blow from every quarter at once, kept rooting up and throwing down tree after tree, and house after house, spreading destruction far and wide.

'Let us only gain St. Rémy and we are safe,' gasped Walter to his pale and trembling companion, who was doing her best to keep on her feet, though continually borne down by the violence of the tornado.

St. Rémy was a little convent on an eminence to the right of the village, hardly fifty yards from the place where they were standing. Walter, with almost superhuman energy, dragged rather than led Gwladys to this their one apparent hope of safety. The door was reached, and in an instant a friendly and loving hand drew them inside, and with difficulty closed the only fragile barrier against that fearful storm.

'Thank God!' exclaimed Gwladys, as she felt herself lovingly kissed by the 'white cornette' who had rescued them from their terrible peril.

'Let us come and thank our Lord,' said the sister simply, leading the way to the little room which served both as school-room and chapel to the community.

There they found the rest of the sisters and their orphans praying earnestly for protection against the danger which threatened them. For Walter had miscalculated the strength of the house which he had fondly looked upon as a sure refuge. It was built of wood, and though proof on ordinary occasions against wind and weather, seemed unlikely to resist long the fury of such a hurricane as that with which they were now visited. Bitterly did he repent having led Gwladys, however unwittingly, into such fearful peril; but it was then too late to do ought but pray. Looking out on the sea below, it appeared like a succession of watery fortifications, the waves dashing madly against the breakers on the point, and hiding the outline of the coast in a blinding mist of spray. Every instant the wind seemed to increase in violence, howling wildly and fiercely round the little convent walls. All of a sudden, Gwladys, who had risen from her knees, and had turned to a window which looked towards the village, uttered an exclamation of horror which made Walter spring to her side. He needed no explanation then of that cry of fear. The swollen river had forced its way through the feeble barriers which ordinarily restrained its bounds, and overflowed the whole place, sapping the foundations of the houses, which were only slender wooden cottages, and bearing them bodily and irresistibly downwards to the sea. What the water began, that the hurricane finished. Roof after roof was blown down on the heads of the occupants, breaking the limbs of some, and killing others outright; whilst the rest were suffocated in a liquid torrent of mud from which there seemed no escape. Every instant the stream became wider and wider. Would it reach St. Rémy? Walter crushed his hands together in mute agony; there seemed no doubt of it. Gwladys, pale as death, watched the apparently resistless enemy as it made rapid but insidious strides nearer and nearer to their frail tenement. What was to be done? To remain was to be exposed to almost certain death, and yet to go out was to brave a furious hurricane which nothing could withstand. They saw the poor people who had endeavoured to leave their falling houses, knocked down flat by the raging cyclone, and then borne away by the impetuous torrents, sinking to appear no more. The only alternative, therefore, seemed to be to stay where they were and endeavour to prepare themselves for the fate which appeared inevitable. The superior, gathering together the weeping children whom she was powerless to save, spoke to them tenderly and yet calmly on submission to the will of God, and acceptance of whatever He might see fit to send. Suddenly a shock, which seemed to shake the cottage to its foundations, made them realise the imminence of their danger. A breach had been made in one of the side walls and the muddy element rushed in fast and thick. Inch by inch it rose and soon covered the floor of the room where they were grouped together. The cries of the children burst forth, only too soon to be stifled by the fast-invading torrent. The sisters knelt in silent prayer. Far other had been their thought when, at the earnest request of the Apostolic Prefect, and the desire of their superiors, they had walked for the last time out of their much loved Mother-house in Paris, and knelt for the last blessing of their venerable Father Superior, before leaving for ever the shores of their native land to devote their lives henceforth to the care of these poor black children. Yet not one faltered or shrunk from the rapidly approaching and terrible death. What matter whether their martyrdom of charity were consummated by the deadly pangs of cholera in an Alexandrian hospital, or by the dagger of a Moslem at Damascus, or by the waterflood in this distant island? They had freely given their lives for Christ's poor, and it had been accepted, and they were only going home a little sooner than they thought. But to Gwladys, with her bright young life flowing strongly in her veins, with hopes yet unfulfilled, and death thought of but as a dim and distant prospect—to her, the moment was terrible. She tried to pray, but fear paralysed her tongue. Confused visions of her home, of her mother, of the Père Marquet, of her faithful Annette, and last, not least, of him, whom she loved but dared not name, chased one another through her brain, and out of the chaos no cry would come but a heart-broken supplication for life and mercy.

And Walter, to him it was maddening. He, in his strong and beautiful manhood, to see her perish and be powerless to save—to be helpless as a child—and she, his angel life, to see her slip away from him ere he had once clasped her to his breast and called her his own; this was agony worse than hell itself! He never for an instant thought of himself; life without Gwladys would be worthless indeed. Winding his strong arms round her slight and drooping form, he bent down to her and whispered, for the first time in his life, passionate words of love into her trembling shrinking ear. Even in the midst of her terror, a joy unspeakable shot through her whole being like an electric spark. At least if she were to die, she would know he had loved her. He who had been her girlish idol, her pride and her joy, her comfort and her stay, he was *hers* in life as in death, hers for evermore! In the exquisite happiness of that revelation, the terrible peril in which they were placed was, for a moment, forgotten. 'Walter, my own Walter!' was all she could murmur, as their eyes met, and for the first time their lips too in tender kisses. But then rushed back, as with a flood, the consciousness of their position. Death seemed inevitable; judgment was at their door. Could they allow themselves to dwell even in thought on human love? Gwladys shuddered as she realised to herself the absorbing nature of their passion in the face of so stern a reality. In broken words she recalled Walter from his dream of love and joy to think of their Lord, before whom it seemed each was so soon to appear. With faltering tongue they united in fervent acts of contrition, faith, and hope in that Higher Love which alone was mighty to save, offering up their human wills to Him to live or to die as He might think fit. And a peace and a strength not their own filled both their hearts with a calm and a confidence unfelt before. But the pause in their agony was but momentary. A sudden and mighty gust of the hurricane, accompanied by an unusual wave of the muddy torrent, burst in upon them, and swept out of the sister's arms the youngest orphan. 'In manus tuas, Domine, commendo spiritum meum.' These words alone echoed through the building as sister after sister was swept away by the relentless flood. Suddenly a more terrible crash than ever was heard. The roof of the convent fell in, burying in its ruins the few remaining inmates. Walter, still clasping Gwladys in his arms, buried up to the neck in water and mud, and unable to move from being wedged in by the wreck of the building, yet contrived to whisper words of comfort, hope, and prayer to the poor girl, who clung convulsively to him as to her only earthly succour. But the hurricane had now spent itself; the storm began to abate, and the humane commander of an English ship, who had weathered the gale by throwing out double anchors and remaining in the shelter of the bay, and who had witnessed from his deck the horrible catastrophe at the village, sent on shore every hand he could spare from his crew to render what assistance they could to the survivors. They arrived first at the convent, and on clearing away a portion of the fallen ruins, discovered, to their joy and surprise, that two of the inmates were still living. The water had by that time risen above Walter's mouth, and for the last hour he had scarcely been able to breathe at all; but he had contrived to raise Gwladys higher up above his head, so that though she had fainted from terror and exhaustion, life was not yet extinct. Tenderly and carefully did the rough sailors extricate the two almost inanimate bodies from the mass of timber which surrounded them, and bore them gently and sadly to the shore. There the ship's doctor, with every restorative that his vessel could afford, hastened to the relief of the sufferers.

Walter was the first to recover consciousness; but the violent pain in his arm, which had been crushed by his successful endeavour to shield Gwladys from a falling beam, caused him to faint away again almost immediately. The injured limb was carefully dressed by the kind surgeon, who next proceeded to examine Gwladys more attentively, for her continued insensibility made him fear some internal injury. Little Margaret, who, with her governess, had taken refuge during the hurricane in one of the many caves which abound on the coast, and who had consequently escaped all hurt, was chafing her cold hands, and sobbing as if her little heart would break at the death-like appearance of her friend. But at last Gwladys opened her eyes, drew a long deep breath, and faintly murmured the word, 'Walter.' It acted on him like an electric shock. He sprung up, and seeing her safe, and surrounded with loving care, fell back again with a 'Thank God!' which came from the very depths of his heart.

'Indeed, they may both well thank God,' exclaimed the doctor, as he went on administering the necessary restoratives. 'Their lives were certainly preserved as by a miracle: the only two saved out of forty souls! And it would have been a pity too,' he went on, soliloquising to himself, as he looked on them both. 'So fair, so young, with all their lives before them ; while as for those who are gone—the Sisters of Charity—why they're sure of heaven, and well out of the scrape of this troublesome weary world; and so are the little children, for that matter!'

Little the good man knew the sorrow that was impending on that fair young head which he was propping gently with a pillow, while in a rough, blunt, yet friendly way, he continued: 'Now, look up a bit, my dear! you'll soon be all right; cheer up, the danger is all over now, and you'll only have given your friends a great fright for nothing.'

Gwladys faintly smiled, and then, glancing towards Walter, exclaimed, 'O, my God! you are hurt! there is blood on your sleeve!'

'It's nothing, only a little squashed,' replied the doctor; 'he may thank his stars he got off so cheap, I assure you! In a few days he will be all right; there are no bones broken!' And so, by a mixture of care and cheerful banter, he had the satisfaction, after half an hour, of seeing his patients able to sit up and take the food he had hastily, yet thoughtfully, prepared for them. Fresh cases of fractured limbs, and still more serious injuries, were being, one by one, brought down by the sailors from the decimated village, and the doctor felt his care was more needed elsewhere. 'Now I must go,' he exclaimed cheerily. 'You're not half bad enough, you see! Stay quiet for an hour or so longer, before you attempt to go home. You came for a picnic, eh! well, it was like to have cost you dear. But "all's well that ends well," you know. No thanks,' he continued hastily, as both Walter and Gwladys were striving to express something of what they felt for his great kindness. 'Why, would you have had me let you die like a dog, without lifting my little finger to help you? No, no! good bye, and take care of yourselves, and say a little prayer for me some day; and ask me to the wedding,' he whispered slily to Gwladys, as he saw the look she cast upon Walter; and, without waiting for an answer, laughingly left the hut.

The presence of little Margaret alone prevented Walter from springing up as soon as the kind old doctor had disappeared, and renewing at Gwladys' feet the passionate declaration of the morning. But their eyes met, and it was enough. Each felt that the other was understood, and under the overwhelming shadow of life's mystery, they entered into a great calm.

How long they would have remained there, drinking in feelings of intensest joy, unknown before, mingled with voiceless but heartfelt thanksgivings for their marvellous deliverance, no one can tell; but they were interrupted by the return of Madame Latour, who, with the practical thoughtfulness which was habitual to her, had arranged everything for their return home with as much care and as little fatigue as circumstances would admit of. And so they started; Gwladys still faint and exhausted, and Walter suffering acutely from his arm; but both in a silent dream of new-found happiness, which had developed a whole world of thought and feeling in them both. As for Gwladys, she felt like a poor little bird who had had her feathers rumpled and bruised and torn in the cold storms of a winter's night, and now found herself in a soft, warm, loving nest, where she would have rest and comfort and joy for evermore.

'What is love? Ask him who lives what is life? Ask him who adores what is God?'

These words had riveted Gwladys' attention in her 'Shelley' some months ago; yet then they were as a sealed book to her; now the hour of the revelation had come; and with it, for the first time, a clearer understanding of that Higher Love of which all earthly affection is but a faint shadow, and from which all that is pure and beautiful emanates, as the heat from the summer sun. Thankfulness, humility, adoration, filled her heart and mind by turns; and all nature wore to her a new and glorified aspect. There was a fresh beauty in the rustling of the trees, and an eloquence in the tongueless wind, and a melody in the flowing stream and the humming of the insects which hovered over it; sounds and sights familiar to her indeed from a child, but now invested with a halo and a charm unfelt before.

There is, in all strong affection, a purity and an intense reality that exalts the individual in whom it has been awakened to the highest pitch of human excellence. It is not a passion; it is a worship, a religion—teaching the sublimest lessons of self-abnegation and sacrifice, and suffering and tender humility, as it feels every instant its unworthiness of the object loved. For, the more tenderly one loves, so much the more does one discover in oneself defects rather than virtues; and in that also, love is like the sun. By daylight our room looks pure and free from dust; but let in a sunbeam, and see what an atmosphere of motes we are living in! What we speak of now is of that close tie, wherein two hearts become mysteriously bound and knit together by a secret influence, which, like the joints of some wonderful puzzle, fit together and in one another only; because they were originally 'made for each other' (as the saying is), and came out of the workshop of the same Divine Artificer. Souls like these love with a pure devotedness which, along its own level, knows neither end nor limit. That which has been there begun and sanctified in life, is continued and perfected hereafter. In its nature it has a something almost sacred, for the Heavenly Father Himself set it in the hearts of His children. When once truly called out, it inspires, as we have before said, a humility and a self-abasement till then unknown; it has a reserve and a modesty and a reverence all its own; it kindles a spirit of generosity and self-sacrifice to which either might before have been a stranger. Like two coals laid side by side, they sympathetically burn together, although each, if left alone, might have remained cold and dark. It incites to noble deeds, and there is no heroism which such love may not call forth. It would give proofs of its reality, if it could, by a thousand ingenuities of suffering and self-sacrifice for the object loved. When once such love has taken root, neither time nor circumstance can affect its growth. Like the oneness of life, so is it, in its kind and order, one and indissoluble. And so, in a maze of happiness and yet of intense humility, Walter and 'Gwladys reached Mrs. Vere's house, and the terrible tale of their hair's-breadth escape was told to eager listeners with glistening eyes. Heartfelt were the thanksgivings offered up that night before the tabernacle to Him who had so mercifully saved them from a fearful and unprepared death. Earnest were the resolutions taken to devote the lives so preserved more heartily to His service. And then Gwladys, after a gush of thankful tears on Mrs. Vere's neck, found herself tucked up in her mosquito-covered bed by loving hands, and soon slept 'the sleep that angels love,' her face beaming with that new beauty which the mixed emotions of the day had created.

Leaving Gwladys to the repose she so much

needed, Mrs. Vere went swiftly to her boy's room. He had thrown himself on his bed, but not to sleep. Wild visions of unspeakable happiness coursed through his brain, and deepened the bright colour on his cheek. His physical pain was altogether absorbed by the thought that it was borne for *her*—his 'life,' —his 'darling life,' as he called her over and over again, the words forming themselves on his lips almost unconsciously, and giving forth no outward sound. And so, as Mrs. Vere sat by his couch and bathed the inflamed and swollen limb with the touch which none but mothers know, Walter told her all. He had never had a secret from her in his life, and now, if he would, he could not. He felt bursting with the strength of his mighty love, and joyful tears ran down his cheeks as he spoke. His mother listened with a joy and thankfulness too deep for words. The wish of her heart was about to be fulfilled, and the remembrance of her own love, never quenched, though hidden in the very depths of her faithful tender heart, quickened her burning sympathy in her boy's confession, and filled up the gaps which the shyness inseparable from intense feeling left in his recital. Long through that eventful night did mother and son talk on the subject so near both their hearts; and even Walter was satisfied at her praises of Gwladys and her thorough appreciation of the wonderful simplicity, tenderness, and goodness, which invested her whole being with such a peculiar charm.

'She will lead you on to all that is noblest and best, my darling, and make your home not brilliant only but blessed,' said Mrs. Vere, after Walter had almost exhausted himself in pouring Gwladys' praises into her loving and sympathising ear. 'But now, my boy,' she continued, 'you must positively rest and try to get some sleep, or fever will come on with this poor crushed arm, and then where will Gwladys be?' she added archly, as Walter, throwing his arms round her neck, exclaimed:

'O, you *darling* mother, how can I be thankful enough for having you both like this? Isn't it wonderful, I say? quite, quite wonderful! It all seems to me, even now, like a dream.'

'Which I hope it soon will be in one sense,' replied Mrs. Vere, laughing. 'Now, not another word. I am going to order you to sleep, as I did when you were a little child,' she added, tenderly, parting the hair from his white forehead, and kissing his open manly brow, while she smoothed his pillow, and having lit his night-light and arranged afresh the cool wet bandages on his injured limb with light and dexterous fingers, softly left him, with his guardian angel, to his rest.

And she herself? Well may we put her last; for an indulgence in her own feelings was a rare luxury for which she had neither time nor physical strength. Her whole life was an effort and a strain. An effort to do her duty bravely, patiently, hopefully, looking to the end, and striving to have no will but His to whom she daily prayed more perfectly to yield up her own.

But Walter's passionate words had roused chords within her which had long lain dormant. The whole recollection of her own intense married happiness, of her husband's tender love, of the bright days of their courtship, their joyous honeymoon, and the still more perfect happiness of the succeeding years of their married life, each of which only seemed to rivet the bond and intensify their mutual love—all this returned upon her with an overwhelming force which seemed to rend her very soul asunder.

'Day and night, he was my breath, and life, and light,' she murmured, as she sat on the little stool which still remained by his armchair, against which so often she had leant her head while reading to him, as they did together night by night, the sacred words of Holy Writ.

Everything had remained untouched in those rooms which had witnessed so many years of their pure and holy love. People wondered and talked, some kindly, some harshly, at her habits in this respect; but to her it mattered little. She went on her way, bearing, suffering, clinging to even the inanimate things which spoke to her of him. But this night it was too much: her self-control broke down altogether, and passionate sobs burst forth from her overcharged and pent-up heart. How surprised those would have been who saw Mrs. Vere in her daily life, with her children, her guests, her dependents, sharing in their interests, their pleasures and their cares, always bright and cheerful, even gay, so that many remarked 'How wonderfully Mrs. Vere had "got over" her trouble'—how surprised these people would have been, I say, if they could have looked in upon her now and seen the real woman, concealed from all eyes but His who knew the burden He had laid upon her, and who alone had given her the strength to bear it with outward bravery. But, after a few moments, her sense of duty returned, and with it a feeling of shame at the momentary self-indulgence.

'How weak and foolish I am,' she exclaimed out loud as she rose and paced rapidly up and down the room, with the knowledge that her impaired strength could no longer bear the past sleepless nights of agony and watching, without utterly incapacitating her for the hard work of the coming day. She opened the window and looked out on the quiet beautiful starry night—those stars which to souls in grief look so pitifully calm and unsympathising sometimes! But, by degrees, the stillness told upon her, a sense of peace, a consciousness of Divine love, stole over her beating, throbbing heart, and with the quiet resignation which had become habitual to her, she knelt again before her crucifix, and there once more accepted the chalice which she had to drink to the dregs.

CHAPTER II.

*Alas! that life should be a dream of love
And not the true reality! alas
That visions from above,
Bright beauteous visions pass,
Even as the shadow of a swallow's wing,
A moment here, then gone again.*

BRIGHT and joyous were the days which followed the eventful scenes detailed in the preceding chapter. Mrs. Vere went at once to Gwladys' father, explaining what had occurred, and asking for his consent to the eventual union of the two children. For children they were still, in one sense; and Mrs. Vere was not anxious that anything more than an engagement between them should be sanctioned for the present. Colonel Murray was not over-well pleased at the turn affairs had taken. He did not fancy losing the only attraction of his home, and Walter's youth seemed to give him sufficient excuse for deferring any decisive answer. But Mrs. Vere could not allow matters to remain on that footing, and so, after a long argument, Colonel Murray having no valid reason to allege against a marriage which promised such eventual comfort and happiness to his child, consented to the union taking place at the end of two years. It was further agreed, that part of the intervening time was to be spent by Walter in a visit to Europe, both to open his mind by the sight of new countries and people, and to cheat his impatience, which was little disposed to wait so long for his promised bride. To Gwladys, however, the delay was of comparatively little importance. She was in no such violent hurry for her marriage! It was enough for present happiness to feel that she was *his*—his ' own, own,' as he called her; to see or write to him every day (Oh! the joy of those letters!); to exchange little presents—one day a bracelet, a true love-knot, of which she gave him the duplicate in a ring; another, a seal, on which he had engraved ' Consola ma non basta,' and she ' Amo e fido;' sharing with him, in fact, every simple pleasure, and the whole coloured with the rainbow tints of youth, and hope, and joy. O! those were indeed happy days for those two bright loving hearts! At other times they would make plans together for his coming travels, of which Gwladys, at first, thought lightly—talking eagerly of the countries and towns and places he would see; London with its smoke and fogs, and Paris with its brilliant gaiety, and Rome with its hallowed associations; and then of the quantities of things he would have to tell her on his return. But ever and anon Walter would come back to that which was far nearer his heart, their future home, their future lives together, which were to be '*one*'—yes one, as the world had never yet seen or known! And then they would make the most delicious castles in the air as to what they would do for their poor people; how a church should be built here, and a school there, and every one in their Utopia be happy and good! Poor children! They were so secure in their happiness, so certain of a bright and unclouded future, that at times Mrs. Vere almost trembled for them; yet she had not the heart, by any warning word of hers, to damp their joy; though an unaccountable dread would sometimes come over her as she looked at them both and thought how any of the thousand accidents of life might shatter that fabric of earthly joy for ever. And so six months passed, and at the time our story opens the hour for Walter's departure was rapidly approaching. Then, and not till then, Gwladys began more seriously to consider how she should be able to bear the terrible separation; how she could get through the weary weeks and months of his absence; how blank and dismal would be the days without a line or a sign of love from him who was her life: and how miserably anxious she should be while waiting for the tardy European posts, which alone could bring her tidings of him. And when those letters did come, they would be so old! Two months old or even more! What might not have happened in that time? It was in this somewhat anxious and dejected mood that the kind Père Marquet found her, when, the little school visited and dinner over, the cool evening air had lured them out again once more to Gwladys' favourite sofa in the verandah, and she was pouring out all her fears and anticipations into his ever-patient ear. He was not altogether sorry that she should have been led to look upon life a little more as it really is: and he took advantage of it to speak to her a few earnest words of trust and faith and submission to God's will—words remembered by Gwladys afterwards with a vividness of which the old man had never dreamed.

The next morning a bright voice calling her under her window, roused Gwladys out of a dream in which she was fancying herself living alone with Walter on a desert island; and springing up and throwing on her dressing gown, while her beautiful hair fell in a shower round her shoulders, she looked out and saw him patiently waiting in the court below.

'You lazy darling!' he exclaimed, 'the sun will soon be up, and the Père Marquet is going

Mass on the Hill. 61

to say mass for us in the little chapel on the hill. Do come quickly!'

'I will,' replied Gwladys; and hastily dressing, was, in a few minutes, standing by his side.

'I wish I could have a picture of you just as you looked at that window with all your hair down,' he exclaimed, as she appeared. 'Why must you turn it up and hide it all like that.'

Gwladys laughed, and slipping her arm into his, they walked quickly up the flowery wooded path, talking, as usual, of their future home and of his mother's tender love and thoughtfulness for them both; when Walter suddenly burst out with:

'How good God is to us, my own Gwladys, is He not? I can hardly understand how I, so unworthy, am so happy, when so many people are so miserable!'

'And we must never forget Him, must we?' rejoined Gwladys, with the unconscious yet fond feeling common to most of us when young and happy, that gratitude would ensure a continuance of such joy. Whereas, God, in His inscrutable wisdom, often deals out crosses instead of happiness even to the most thankful of His creatures, until they have learned that these very crosses are but blessings in disguise. O! those beautiful tropical mornings! when the air is yet fresh, and cool, and pure; and the fire-flies are still glimmering in the dewy grass; and the flowers are just bursting into fresh bloom and sweetness; and the birds are waking each other to sing their morning hymn of praise; and the dawn is struggling with the night, and every moment gaining the day! It was scarcely light when Gwladys and Walter reached the mountain top, but already a large congregation, chiefly of negroes, was assembled in the little church, to whom the Père Marquet addressed a few loving words on the feast of the day. The Holy Sacrifice followed, which Gwladys had begged Walter to make a Mass of Thanksgiving, and when both partook of the Bread of Life. After which the three walked back joyfully, yet calmly, to the cottage, and their mutual love seemed to have

Mission of Walter and Père Marquet. 63

acquired a fresh force from the shadow of that Higher Love of which they had been made partakers.

The cheerful breakfast over, and all Gwladys' pets having been duly fed and attended to, the good old Père Marquet rose to go, asking Walter to accompany him to an outlying mission, whither his widely-scattered duties led him on that day. Gwladys, in the meanwhile, was very busy packing up a little parcel of clothes which she wished to send to the poor children of this distant station; and then entrusting it to Walter, said gaily:

' Now, you must take great care of this, and not forget it and carry it all the way home again, as you did last time, you bad Walter! And take care of dear Père Marquet, too, across the ford,' she added more earnestly, ' you know it is swollen after these heavy rains, and is dangerous in parts.' And so, with a loving kiss from her betrothed, and a tender blessing from the Père Marquet, the two gentlemen rode off, Gwladys watching them from the steps of the verandah, the sun lighting up her head,

and her white dress glistening against the
dark green background of evergreens behind
her. And Walter, turning round at the top of
the hill to kiss his hand to her once more, saw
her thus *for the last time* in her island home.

An unusual feeling of sadness and depression stole over Gwladys when she was left
alone. Was it a presentiment of coming
sorrow? Whatever it was she was ashamed
of it, and resolved to rouse herself vigorously
to overcome it by setting about her daily
duties. So, taking her hat from its peg, she
set off for her school, and there was soon deeply
engaged in teaching her little black and brown
protégés the mysteries of reading and writing,
promising them a treat if, in a few weeks, they
had succeeded in mastering the unwelcome
tasks. By the time the children's play-hour
came, she had recovered her spirits; and
trotting gaily home, filled a little basket with
soup and sick comforts, and then set off again
to see some of her poor people in the cottages
on the hill beyond the house, with a bright
word and a kind look for each and all, long

remembered by those on whose ear her footstep would never again fall. With one old woman, who was her special favourite, she stayed some time, reading out loud to her portions of the 'Imitation,' which was her favourite book.

'Why do you always choose out this particular chapter?' she asked of her old friend that day, when begged by her for the twentieth time to read 'The Way of the Cross.'

'Ah, my dear young lady,' replied the poor woman, 'you have yet to learn the sweetness of *that* way, and God grant that it may be many years first,' she added, looking at the fair young face beside her, on which sorrow and care had, as yet, left no trace. Gwladys was unconsciously saddened by her words, and read that beautiful portion of that matchless book with more attention and thought than usual. How often this scene and those words recurred to her in after years, when she had indeed trodden that rough and rugged road, and learned the secret which then was hid from her eyes! But as yet, all was bright to her: and her sick people visited, she was trotting gaily home with an empty basket and a glad heart, when, on turning into the path which led to the cottage, she was startled by meeting her father, and with him two or three gentlemen, among whom she discovered, to her great annoyance, Lord William de Tracey, whose open and somewhat insolent attentions to her on a previous visit had roused the anger which she had expressed in those few words to Père Marquet the evening before. She was hastily passing them with a hurried kiss to her father, when Lord William, laying his hand on her arm, exclaimed:

'Whither so fast, lady fair? It is not so often that we see a face like yours that we can afford to let it go!'

Gwladys coloured up to the roots of her hair and looked imploringly at her father for protection, but he only laughed, and said:

'Come, Gwladys, you must do the honours of our home to these friends of mine. I hope you have got a good dinner for us, for our ride has made us as hungry as hunters.'

'O! I must go and see about it,' replied Gwladys, seizing the opportunity for escape; and coldly bowing to Lord William, who had released her arm, she sped like a frightened hare into the house. Arrived there, she flew up to her old nurse's room, and burst into a violent flood of tears.

Annette, greatly astonished, asked her 'What in the world was the matter?' on which poor Gwladys poured out on the loving woman's neck her troubles and her fears, and asked her if it would not be possible for her to plead a headache that evening, as an excuse for not appearing at dinner.

Annette shook her head. 'I fear it would be impossible, Miss Gwladys, quite impossible! You know how angry your papa would be; and he has a particular reason, I am afraid, from what I hear downstairs, for wishing to keep on good terms with that Lord William. More's the pity! Well,' she continued, more cheerily, to her nursling, 'you must keep up a brave heart, my dear, and let him see that you don't like his admiration, and then, perhaps, he will not venture to annoy you.' But, in her own mind, Annette had no such hope, so that it was with great anxiety and no little sadness and anger, too, in her heart, that the faithful servant saw Gwladys go downstairs that evening, looking prettier and more pure than ever, in her snowy-white muslin, with no ornament, save some fresh jessamine in her luxuriant soft brown hair.

The presence of the servants during dinner saved Gwladys from any very marked attentions on the part of her hateful guest, though his rank compelled her to take his arm on going in. But she saw, with dismay, the deference paid to him by her father, and his evident anxiety that she should please and put him in good humour. Her only cause of unmixed thankfulness was, that Walter was gone, that Walter was not there; she felt his spirit never could have borne it, and that some serious quarrel or scene would have been the consequence. Even with that reflection, however, she thought the dinner would never end, and as soon as possible, when the dessert had been put on the table, she rose to make her escape.

'By Jove! that's a lovely child of yours, Colonel Murray,' exclaimed Lord William, as she left the room. 'A little shy and all that, wants a little breaking-in perhaps, but wonderfully pretty, certainly,' he continued, as if half to himself. 'What a "fureur" she would make in a London drawing-room!'

Colonel Murray looked gratified, and pressed more wine upon his guest, which he, for reasons of his own, declined, being determined that night to keep sober.

'No, I thank you, I had enough of that yesterday evening, when you made me as drunk as an owl, and cleaned me out completely in consequence. But I'm going to have my revenge to-night, you know,' he added, with an evil smile at his host, who winced at the exposure of his trap of the night before, and said, in a tone which he tried to make jocose:

'Well, if you were, as you say, "as drunk as an owl," I was more than "half seas over," so we were well matched, I think!'

Lord William gave a long low whistle, expressive of incredulity, and presently said: 'Well, mayn't we go to the ladies? I have a wish to see a little more of that fair girl of yours before the night's work begins.'

Colonel Murray, to do him justice, had no excuse, if he would, for keeping his guest from the drawing-room that evening, although even he could not but feel some remorse at the persecution to which he knew he was exposing his child from the hands of so unscrupulous and unwelcome an admirer. All he could do was to keep tolerably near her, although Lord William respected him too little to make his presence of much avail in checking his persistent attentions. At last, to Gwladys' intense relief, one of the other gentlemen, pitying her evident distress, proposed to play a game of chess with her, under the shelter of which she contrived to escape his further importunities, till the servants, bringing in the supper tray, gave her a pretext for leaving the room.

And then began, what Lord William had justly called, the 'work of the night;' heavy play for heavy stakes, on which the very existence of the principals depended. And far into the night that work continued, the intense silence only broken by the rustling of the cards as they were being shuffled, or by the occasional tearing up of parts of a pack, or by the crackling sound of the breaking of the seals of a new one. The lookers-on were equally mute. A grind of the teeth, a twitch of the hands, or the echo of a dry tongue trying to moisten still dryer lips, these were the only signs of life given by the gamblers during those fearful hours. And as the day broke, Colonel Murray rose, and staggered from the table a ruined man.

'*Give me your daughter, and the whole shall be cancelled,*' hissed, rather than whispered, Lord William in his ear. Yes! it was for that he had been playing all that terrible night, it was for that he had kept sober, it was for that he had vowed, with an oath, to get Colonel Murray into his power. He had fallen madly, passionately in love with Gwladys at first sight, and he had sworn to make her his own. And now he had *won* her. He knew the base selfishness of the man with whom he had to deal, and he never doubted but that he was sure of his prize. And so, with his whole frame in a state of excitement and exultation impossible to describe, he poured out a tumbler of brandy, drank it off on the spot, and then threw himself on the nearest bed with the fierce determination to quench all feelings of pity or remorse, and to leave no stone unturned to attain his end.

And Colonel Murray! Bad and hardened as the miserable man was, he could not without a shudder reflect on the horrible bargain proposed to him. To sell his pure and innocent child to a man like that, to force her to break her plighted troth to another, and that other one whom she so fondly loved — no, it was impossible! Sooner would he beg his bread! And yet, what was the alternative? Not only utter misery, absolute ruin, but dishonour and disgrace; his name branded for ever among his fellow-men, his future life like that of Cain! Either course was unbearable. He paced in agony up and down his room, cursing his own folly, cursing his fate, cursing him who had laid this plot for him and lured him to his ruin. Suicide occurred to him, and he took out his pistols; but he was too much of a coward for that: he had not even the courage to be a villain! Suddenly a numbness came over him—a strange wild sensation as if he were going to die—his head reeled—and with a cry which roused the whole house, he fell heavily forwards in a fit.

When he recovered consciousness, he found that he had been bled, and that a strange doctor was standing by his bedside, while Gwladys, anxiously watching his every movement, was tenderly bathing his forehead, which had been bruised in his fall. All her fear of her father vanished when she saw him thus prostrate: she only thought of his danger, and of what she could do to alleviate and help him. As his eyes rested on her, a full recollection of the events of the past night came back upon him, and with a deep groan, he turned away his head to the other side.

'He will do now,' said the doctor to Gwladys, 'if you can keep him very quiet, and not let him have anything to vex or distress him. This fit can only have been caused by some great shock, or by acute mental distress. *Any fresh excitement would kill him.*'

With these words, he took his leave, after sundry directions as to his patient's treatment and diet; and Gwladys and her father were left alone.

A horrible and fiendish hope shot through the mind of the miserable man, as he heard the doctor's concluding words; that Gwladys' fears might be so worked upon, as to induce her to sacrifice herself for him. He knew her generosity of soul, her unselfish devotion, her high sense of filial duty. Once make her feel that his *life* depended on her self-immolation, and he felt he was safe. But first he thought he would try what could be done with Lord William himself, and if no compromise could be arrived at by which to escape from this terrible alternative. Taking advantage, therefore, of Gwladys having left the room for a short time, he sent a message to Lord William, to say he wished to speak to him. Lord William came, sufficiently sober to be shocked at the haggard face of the man he had robbed, and well-nigh murdered; but nothing would induce him to waver an inch in his purpose, to possess himself of Gwladys by fair means or by foul. The wretched father, finding all appeal to his generosity to be in vain, detailed his plan, which was, to work upon her feelings of duty, so as to get her voluntarily to make the sacrifice, and then to consummate it with such speed and secresy as to give her no time for reflection or repentance, and her friends no chance of interference on her behalf. Lord William listened eagerly to a proposal which tallied so perfectly with his own wishes. He was anxious to start the following day by the Australian steamer, and if he could only obtain the necessary licence in time, the marriage might be solemnised in the consul's house early the following morning, and Gwladys could be conveyed directly afterwards on board the steamer. So these two worthy colleagues concocted and discussed this devilish scheme, and Lord William instantly started off for Port Louis to carry it into execution. By night, the terrible preparations were made; the licence had been obtained. What will not ready money do? The berths on board the steamer were taken, and notice given to the consul that they would be the following morning at his house. Nothing remained, therefore, but to induce the victim to accept her fate; and from that task Colonel Murray shrunk as from death itself. But Lord William would brook no delay; and so, when the evening came, and Gwladys was again alone by her father's bedside, he told her all. He implored her to save him; he represented to her the hopeless misery, disgrace, and ruin which her refusal would entail upon him. He conjured her, by all the heroism that was up some actual work, which should so engross her mind as to leave her no time for morbid misery. Mrs. Levin warmly seconded her in this wise resolve, encouraging her also in reading a variety of books bearing on the new country which was about to be her home, and of which there was a good supply on board: so that by the time they arrived at Sydney, her natural buoyancy and hopefulness of character, combined with the earnest religious impressions instilled into her by the Père Marquet, enabled her to face the future with more courage than she would a month before have thought possible. And all her courage was needed; for the prospects before them on landing were of the gloomiest description.

Although Australia may justly be termed the El Dorado of the sober, industrious working man, it is the reverse for the spendthrift gentleman, who, with no idea of manual labour, and a fanciful belief in his own omnipotence, finds himself speedily reduced to the very verge of starvation.

'What the devil am I to do?' exclaimed

Lord William to his young wife, when, after about six weeks of vain attempts to obtain some situation as clerk, or warehouse overseer, —which, to do him justice, he had at first tried for—he returned disappointed and disgusted to their comfortless lodgings. 'There is nothing to be done in this d——d country; and those villains cleared me out of my last shilling yesterday, at the club! Why don't you answer me?' he continued, with increased irritation, as Gwladys remained silent. 'What's the good of a woman if she can't help a man in a pinch like this?'

'I was going to suggest to you trying to leave the town,' she replied, mastering the rising colour which his harsh words had roused. 'Mr. Levin told me that up the country, in the bush, that is, you might perhaps get some situation as assistant overseer; and living, at any rate, would be cheaper.'

'That's all very well,' replied her husband; 'but how are we to get there? and how pay for these wretched lodgings, I should like to know, unless your canting friend there will help us a bit? But that's always the way with your '*good* people,' he added, with a sneer. 'They are full of charity and fine words as long as it costs them nothing.'

Gwladys checked the angry retort that was rising to her lips, and calmly saying, 'I will go out and try and see, and consult with her,' she left her comfortless apartment to seek her friend.

A great contrast to her own miserable home was the bright, cheery, sunny morning room into which, half an hour after, she was ushered. Mr. Levin was a banker, and, with his wife and three children, lived in a pretty villa just outside the town, but near enough for him to go in daily to his counting-house. He had taken a great fancy to Gwladys, from the first moment his wife had introduced her to him when they met on the crowded wharfs on the day of landing, and all he had heard of her sufferings and present position had increased his interest in her; but it was only for her sake, and to spare her feelings, that he could keep up the semblance of civility towards her husband, whose character he read at a glance, and for whom he felt a contempt which even exceeded his dislike. Gwladys instinctively felt this, and that to ask him to recommend Lord William for employment would be hopeless. She trusted, however, to his influence to put them in the way of hearing of some vacant situation for which he might apply in the ordinary way, and in this she was not mistaken. An overseer was needed for a run 250 miles up the country; and although the pay was small, and the station did not sound very inviting, still Gwladys jumped at it, if only as a means of getting her husband away from the low set with whom he had become acquainted since his arrival at Sydney. The delicate generosity of Mr. Levin, who suspected their financial difficulties, relieved Gwladys from the humiliation of asking for help. Towards the end of the following week they started for their new home, with some sinking of heart on Gwladys' part, at the prospect of a hitherto untried life, alone with so uncongenial a companion; and yet, with the buoyancy of youth, flattering herself that things would turn out better than she expected, and that a country life would anyhow be more endurable than the struggle with poverty in a large capital. Before their departure, she had been comforted by a few loving lines from Mrs. Vere, in answer to her heart-breaking note of farewell to Walter. It ran as follows:—

'My poor Child,—Far be it from me to reproach you for the misery which has fallen upon us all, and of which you, I fear, will have the heaviest portion to bear. Believe only this, that we can never cease to love and to pray for you. Day and night you are our one thought. Walter wished to write himself; but he has yielded to my entreaties that he would let me take his place. You know well that he can *never change*. I think it is probable he will leave me for a time, and join his uncle in India; but nothing is yet settled. The Père Marquet sends you his blessing, and desires me to say he has never forgotten you in his prayers. Do not talk of asking for our forgiveness, my poor darling! *we know all!*

May God comfort you and strengthen you, and give you His peace.

'Your ever affectionate,

'E. Vere.'

Travelling in Australia, thirty years ago, was a far different thing from what it is now, when civilisation has crept on with giant strides, and the first sheep and first lamb imported in the memory of men now living, have multiplied to such an extent that the difficulty at present is to know what to do with the quantity of meat produced!

A two-wheeled spring cart, covered with canvas, and a dray drawn by oxen, carrying the articles of furniture necessary for the nightly halt, together with the universal tin pot and pannikin, and the bags of flour, brown sugar, tea and bacon, which formed their commissariat, a store-keeper, a drayman, and three ticket-of-leave convicts assigned to them as servants, composed the caravan with which Gwladys and her husband started for their new home.

Their route led them slowly through a slightly wooded and rising plain towards the Blue Mountains, the first day's halt being at Paramatta, the summer residence of the governor, and the resort of the wealthier settlers during the hot season.

Nothing could be more miserable than the appearance of the country in the 'clearing' they had passed after leaving what the aborigines call the 'big smoke,' or town of Sydney. Slab huts half tumbling down, occupied by drunken women and ragged children, heaps of ashes, broken bottles, and old casks scattered round the doors; with ugly blackened stems or stumps of trees which the first settlers had contented themselves with cutting down about a yard from the ground to save themselves the trouble of grubbing up the roots, and chain-gangs working on the dusty track, guarded by overseers with loaded muskets, whose villanous countenances made Gwladys shudder as she passed; the emigrant's first impressions were certainly not favourable! But at Paramatta they found an unusually clean and tidy resting-place, the verandah of the little inn being covered with vines and jessamine, and surrounded by a garden in which the aloe, pomegranate, and oleander were mingled with mandarin oranges, and shaded by mulberry and fig trees, so that poor Gwladys could have almost fancied she had returned to her old home. Early the next morning they crossed the Nepean, a fine and rapid river, their cart and dray being ferried over on a species of raft, which landed them safely on what are called the 'Emu Plains' (guiltless though they may be of emus!), through which they travelled pleasantly enough until they reached the foot of Lapstone Hill, where the ascent of the mountains begins. A more sandy, ill-devised, and worse constructed road never existed than that which our emigrants had now to follow. We talk of distances 'as the crow flies,' and that much maligned bird seems to have been the main engineer in the tracing out of this particular track, which leads right across a chain of mountains with manifold spurs, involving incessant descents and ascents, at one time down steep and precipitous ravines where the poor beasts could hardly keep their footing, then crossing what are dried-up beds of torrents at one season, and still more perilous rushing water at the other; and then laboriously ascending again a new ridge, as if it were for the very purpose of adding to the fatigue and weariness of the traveller. At first, however, the strangeness and wildness of the scenery had a charm for Gwladys; in the crags and recesses of the rocks grew endless flowers and shrubs new to her in form and colour; while the 'waratah,' with its crimson trumpet-shaped blossoms threw a kind of shade across their path, and the song of the bell-bird near the water, and the bright blue and pink lories higher up (that most beautiful of the parrot tribe), gave a tropical look and character to the scenery. But soon flowers and birds and herbage of all kinds were left far behind. Tall gum trees, monotonous in form and colour, alone clothed the arid mountain sides, trees whose leaves placed vertically with their edges towards the stem give no shade, and might rather be called ever-brown than ever-green! while the inmates of the carts were jolted almost to death by the 'jumpers,' as the slabs are called, which are thrown roughly over the gaps and holes continually occurring in the ill-kept road.

The country was only just recovering from a recent drought which had left behind it grievous marks of devastation. Scanty and poor was the forage for their weary cattle; the forest was silent and deserted by birds or animals, and at times the solitude became almost appalling. Skeletons of beasts of burden, fragments of broken carts, bleached bones of oxen and of men, lined the desolate track, and added not a little to the melancholy around. Still, the sky was cloudless—heavenly blue by day, or richly illuminated towards evening by the setting sun; and the distant horizon before them, seen from the tops of the ridges which they were crossing, with the fantastic shapes of the crags (like the Val di Bove of Etna), sometimes weird-looking and naked, sometimes smooth and wooded, gave an ever-new aspect to the landscape, although the pleasant illusion was often dispelled on a nearer approach.

Thus the little caravan plodded wearily on, day by day, always hoping in the morrow, which was to bring them an easier road and less exhausting toil. But the brighter morrow never came; and Gwladys' heart grew sick and faint at expectations for ever frustrated. They used to start a little before sunrise, halting in the middle of the day for a few hours to escape the rays of the burning sun, and then starting on again till evening brought them to a green patch of grass by a tiny rivulet or creek, in which they could fix their night's encampment.

Who can tell the pleasure to a weary traveller in an unknown country, which is new and enigmatic in every bearing, and where the distances seem to lengthen out in proportion to one's fatigue; who can express, I say, the delight of rounding a point and coming upon the welcome smoke of the camp-fire, telling of rest and food after the struggles and fatigues of the long and weary day?

Civilised life at home, with all its appliances of comfort and refinement, knows nothing of these enjoyments, or of the luxury of stretching out one's cramped limbs on a camp-bed when too weary to do more (like an animal) than eat and sleep! Had her companion been more congenial to her, the novelty of this life would have delighted Gwladys; but there was no response in his mind to any pure or natural pleasures, and still less to the higher aspirations of hers. And so, when the mid-day halt came, and Lord William sat down to drink and sleep, Gwladys would wander through the wild ravines, with her ever-ready pencil and sketch-book, to try and carry away some lasting reminiscence of this her first journey; or else she would sit alone thinking, praying, trying hour by hour to accept her fate with submission and cheerfulness if not with absolute inward calm, and thus acquiring unconsciously a more personal knowledge, of Him who alone could satisfy the needs of her loving heart.

So, uneventfully, passed the first few days.

One evening, however, just as they had settled themselves in their encampment for the night, the low growl of their dog gave warning of the advent of a stranger, and from the thicket of underwood and scrub which fringed their camping-ground, emerged a woman like an apparition. She was tall and handsome, gipsy-like in gait and dress, and with a look of stern resolve and pain in her dark eyes and firmly-cut mouth. She walked up to the little group by the camp-fire, who were too much surprised to speak, and there stood motionless for awhile, as if hesitating what to do. Presently her eye fell upon Gwladys' tender face and questioning kindly looks, which seemed at once to decide and reassure her. She advanced firmly and quickly to her side, and then and there poured out her tale of anxiety and sorrow, imploring their assistance for a dying man, lying in a hopeless condition in a gully not far distant, and with impassioned words and gestures besought the aid she was powerless to give. When she had finished, she remained perfectly still, her hands tightly clasped, with her black expressive eyes fixed on Gwladys' face, pleading even more irresistibly than her words. Gwladys sprung from her seat and looked imploringly at her husband for consent. He, weary of the monotony of the journey, and unconsciously touched by the beautiful expression which the glow of charity had kindled in her face, gave an unreluctant assent to the stranger's petition, and even volunteered to accompany them to the place where the sick man lay. Gwladys, hastily collecting all the medical comforts with which the thoughtful kindness of Mrs. Levin had supplied her, and ascertaining from the woman that the sick man was badly wounded by fire arms, hurried after her guide to the fatal spot. She could hardly keep pace with the rapid strides of that anxious devoted spirit, who tore her way, regardless of scrub and thorns, over the roughest ground for nearly an hour, when they reached a cave, where, on a couch of neatly and carefully arranged fern-leaves, was stretched a man motionless, and apparently half dead.

Close to him, holding his already cold hand, crouched a girl perfectly beautiful in face and form, whose eyes were fixed on the apparently sinking sufferer, whom she was fanning with a palmetto leaf, but with an expression of calm, mute, concentrated agony which went straight to Gwladys' heart. Suddenly, the sick man opened his eyes, and a shudder passed over him as he caught sight of Lord William. But Gwladys bent forward and whispered into his ear a few words of love and kindness. 'Do not fear, we are friends; we are come to help you,' she said. And at the sound of her voice, the wild look in his features relaxed, and he breathed a deep sigh of relief and thankfulness. The girl sprung from the corner where she was kneeling, and instinctively threw her arms round Gwladys' neck, who seemed to her as an angel of help. The sufferer endeavoured to articulate some incomprehensible words through his parched lips; but his state required little explanation. His left arm was terribly lacerated, and there was a serious wound in the breast on the left side, caused by a rifle ball, which demanded instant care. Gwladys was used to illness. The Père Marquet had given her simple instructions what to do in cases of emergency, and had taught her not to shrink from the sight of blood or pain, if thereby she could relieve the sufferer. To fetch some water; to wash and dress the gaping and neglected wounds; to make a splint out of the bark of a young gum tree near at hand; all this was the work of a few moments. With skilful and dexterous hand she bandaged the wounded limb, and then administered a restorative draught which had a magical effect. After about an hour the sick man fell into a quiet and refreshing sleep, from which he woke so much better that he was able to express in a few fervent words his gratitude for the timely aid he had received. His language betrayed that he was a gentleman, and Gwladys was more and more puzzled at the apparent contradiction between his outward circumstances and his evident gentle breeding. By her earnest entreaties, Lord William was induced to delay his journey for a few days;

and when the wounded man understood that it was done for his sake, his voice faltered, and the squeeze of his firm but delicate hand, and the moisture in his eye, told of feelings deeper than words could say. Out of delicacy, both Lord William and Gwladys abstained from asking him any questions as to his name or antecedents. The last day of their visit they found him up and dressed, proud and erect in bearing, resolute in looks, with a countenance belonging to other climes and another condition of life. He stood with his young and beautiful wife by his side, she holding by the hand a little boy, their only child; and the three together formed a group which would have delighted the heart of a painter. Who were they? From whence had they come? What had brought on the bloody strife? and with whom? All this remained a mystery. They separated as strangers, never to meet again in this world, but with a consciousness on the one part that an act of true love had been performed, and on the other that it was deeply appreciated and gratefully acknowledged.

Resuming their march, which this little episode had interrupted, our emigrants found themselves suddenly in a romantic pass, a huge barrier of rocks seeming to close the onward path, till a sudden turn in the road showed them a narrow gorge, through which they drove, with a high wall of crags on either side. Emerging from this pass, they came in sight of the beautiful valley of Clwydd, with its bright glistening stream and its sweet-scented flowering shrubs, around the stems of which the violet pea-shaped blossoms of the native indigo climbed in graceful profusion. Crossing this valley, which is connected with the Victoria Pass by a fine arch and embankment, the party found themselves again ascending a steep and precipitous range of hills, called 'Hassan's Walls,' their path shaded by the grass tree, with its long narrow sharp leaves and heavy clustering foliage, looking at a distance like a miniature palm. Here they experienced for the first time the ill-effects of the khamseen or hot wind, which, blowing violently from the north-west, arrested their progress, and threatened destruction to both man and beast.

Everything green was scorched and withered up. Fine crops of barley and oats appeared in a few hours absolutely blackened by the breath of this terrible air, thin and shrivelled up into a charred and formless mass. The sky itself was cloudless, but the atmosphere lurid and reddish, more fiery than the fiery sun itself; while through the air floated minute particles of earth and blinding dust, parching the lips, affecting both eyesight and respiration, and producing upon the whole animal frame a singular and disastrous depression of the vital powers. Several days elapsed before the party were sufficiently recovered to enable them to proceed on their journey, and to face the road before them, which lay across the last spurs of the Blue Mountains, and was proportionately steep and difficult of ascent. The rocks were of a splintery bluish-coloured slate, devoid of trees or shrubs, and gloomy in the extreme. On and on they toiled, up the precipitous sides of

Mount Lambey, till, the summit being reached, they were rewarded by the sight of the fertile plains of Bathurst and the silvery line of the Macquarie River, dividing in its deep channel the little township of that name into two distinct and separate stations. Striking off, however, by a bye-road, towards the Liverpool Plains, which was the nearest way to their destination, they were suddenly surrounded by a group of bushrangers, who sprung from a thicket to their left, and in an instant disarmed and overpowered their little caravan. Even had the attack been less unexpected, their numbers made resistance hopeless: so that Lord William and his men were unresistingly bound, and then marched off, with Gwladys, by an unknown region and through an almost impenetrable scrub to the camp, where their ultimate fate was to be decided.

After many hours of weary march, they reached at sunset a gloomy spot, where the bushrangers decided to halt for the night. The character of the locality did not tend to raise the spirits of our travellers. Silence had

The Capture of the Travellers. 113

been enforced by their captors; remonstrances were worse than useless, and they had nothing to do but to obey. To Gwladys herself some rough courtesy had been shown by the leader of the band, who had placed her on a sure-footed pony, and seized the bridle whenever the precipitous nature of the road rendered riding a matter of some peril. But she was so spent with fatigue on arriving at their resting-place, that even the deep anxiety and uncertainty as to their fate could not prevent her dropping asleep at once on the rug which had been laid for her by the camp fire. Lord William, in the meantime, was desired to write down their names and those of his men—to state from whence he came and whither he was going—and likewise to make out an exact inventory of his property, which was to be transferred to his captors. All protests or supplications were in vain—instant compliance seemed their only chance of mercy.

As soon as the required papers had been duly written and signed, they were handed over to three or four of the leading men of the band, who instantly started off from the camp in an opposite direction, carrying the papers with them. The rest remained with loaded muskets to watch over their prisoners, who were now unbound, so as to preclude the least possibility of their escape. Two nights and one whole day were spent in this manner, and the mental distress and suffering of the party hourly increased. At last, at daybreak of the second day, three men arrived in the camp as messengers from their chief, and after a whispered consultation with the rest, the oldest amongst them advanced courteously to Gwladys and announced to her that he was the bearer of their release, adding his deep regret for the inconvenience and hardships to which they had been exposed, and restoring to them intact every article included in the inventory. The band vied with one another in kindness and courtesy, and urged upon their men the acceptance of all that was best in the camp by way of food, as well as several presents which were contained in two sacks brought by the messengers.

Whence arose this sudden change of conduct—this most unexpected kindness? Gwladys' thoughts reverted instantly to the wounded man in the mysterious cave, and rightly conjectured that he had thus repaid their act of charity. One pledge only was demanded of the party, that of secresy as to the whole circumstances of the capture and release, and especially as to the spot where the deed had been effected. Joy at the *dénouement* of an adventure which had threatened such disastrous consequences made Lord William give the promise required with the utmost alacrity; and the bushrangers instantly prepared to escort them back to the route they had so unwillingly left two days before. But to all Lord William's questions as to their chief and the motive of his generosity, they returned no answer; simply saying that they were obeying orders and had nothing further to communicate. But the tender care they took of Gwladys revealed a more than common link which bound these rough men to her, and deepened the sympathy which she could not help feeling for human beings sc misguided, and who had been led, perhaps from no grave fault of their own, to a career of danger and crime, of which the end could only be suffering, ignominy, and death.

After a few days of quiet journeying through a somewhat monotonous and parched-up country, the little party reached a more pastoral and promising land, interspersed with tiny creeks and running water, with patches of verdure and picturesque nooks, each more tempting than the other for the evening's encampment. At one of these welcome oases, while congratulating themselves on the danger they had escaped and the difficulties they had overcome, they were surprised by the unexpected appearance of a gentleman in his dog-cart, who had perceived their little camp, and came to ask permission to join them for the night.

A guest in the bush is always a godsend, and nothing could be more welcome or agreeable than their actual visitor, who was a crown commissioner of the Liverpool Plains, for which they were bound, and who could consequently give them endless information of the kind most interesting to them at that moment. He might be called a bey or sheik of the district, so entirely were all things subject to his will. An exchange of questions on topics of mutual interest, with reminiscences of home and the mother country—to which all English hearts instinctively turn, no matter how distant may be the place of their pilgrimage—made the evening pass only too rapidly. And then the supper! It exceeded every one's expectations. The store-keeper, still joyous at the recollection of his recent liberation, had surpassed himself in the culinary art, and had added to their usual fare the preserved meats, wines, and delicacies which the courtesy of the bush-rangers had pressed upon them. What particularly excited the admiration of their guest, who seemed a 'bon vivant,' was the quality of ham served.

'It is delicious!' he exclaimed, having helped himself to a second edition, 'Westphalia, certainly! It must have come from the same store as mine, but of which, I am sorry to say, I was robbed by the bushrangers a few days ago. The rascals, not content with the hams, carried off all my preserved meats, wines, and liqueurs! But I am now on my way to Sydney to get the governor to augment the police station and avenge the outrage. The band is formidable,' he added, 'and they had a brush with the police the other day near the Vale of Clwydd, when their chief, an English baronet, after heroic acts of personal valour, was killed. (Gwladys glanced at Lord William, but was silent.) They are now on this side of the Blue Mountains, and committing robberies and depredations hardly to be credited or imagined.'

Little their visitor knew what was passing in Gwladys' mind at that moment, and how well she was acquainted with those of whom the commissioner spoke so bitterly! But she kept her own counsel, and only prayed in her heart that the brave chief and his beautiful child-wife might yet be spared to regain their place in society, and escape the terrible retribution which she shuddered to contemplate as their possible fate. For it is not only the bad who are driven to take pleasure in this wild life: injustice, harshness, and wrong have made more Robin Hoods than deliberate love of crime; and of the real generosity and nobility of soul that are sometimes found in the outlaw's breast, let Poland and Sicily at this moment tell.

And now their weary travel was soon to draw to a close, and the evening of the following day saw them approaching the long wished-for station.

It required all their previous experiences of hardship and rough accommodation, not to be disappointed with the aspect of the place which was to be their future home. On the top of a little eminence stood a bark hut, composed of four upright and two transverse posts, and a species of stringy bark filling up the interstices of the walls; while the roof was composed of the same material, with no pretence at ornament or decoration, or even beauty of proportion. This was the principal habitation; the master's hut. At the back was an immense wool-shed, floored with narrow slabs of wood, to protect the fleeces from the dirt, but otherwise constructed in the same way as the dwelling-house. Four or five slab-houses for the workmen, of the rudest description, and a large stock-yard, completed the so-called 'station.' The trees had been roughly cleared, with no attempt at picturesque effect, or any idea of the value of shade to the inmates of the huts, and the grass grew in rough tussocks, at such wide distances from one another, that it is calculated that four acres are required for the feeding of a single sheep. Gwladys' artistic and tropical taste was pained by the look of the whole place, which a group of evergreen cypress and cactus-shaped Banksia behind the house made even more lugubrious and funereal. But she was not one to yield to more than momentary depression; and so, hastily leaving their rough vehicle, she set to work vigorously to unpack various articles of furniture, so that by night the bare-floored hut had assumed a look of comfort and of home in a manner which astonished Lord William, unaccustomed to the magical effect of a woman's hand in such arrangements and under such circumstances.

Outside, the prospect was certainly not inviting. A rough four-rail fence, with 'sliprails,' as a substitute for a gate, enclosed the so-called 'orchard;' but a drunken predecessor in the station had let everything go to rack and ruin, and the cattle had entirely destroyed the mulberry and apple-trees, of which only a few gnarled branches remained to tell the tale of former produce. There was no attempt at a garden; while, close to the edge of the 'clearing,' rose up the impenetrable ' bush,' i.e. low marshy land overgrown with scrub, full of rank and prickly vegetation, the wild vine clambering over the whole, and impeding the progress of the pedestrian in every direction. The vicinity of the hut was strewn with broken hurdles, strips of bullocks' hide, and bits of sheepskin, which the previous occupiers had not thought it worth their while to remove.

Gwladys' heart sank within her the next morning when, Lord William having started at sunrise to accompany the surveyor to the out-stations, which were to be equally under his care, she was left alone to make the best of these unpromising materials. A fresh dread likewise came over her;—the cheapness of intoxicating liquors, and the scenes of drunkenness they had witnessed at the wayside inns on their road, convinced her that they had come to almost the worst country in the world to cure Lord William's besetting sin; and her apprehensions were confirmed by the talk of the men about the station, who looked upon the roadside 'grog-shop' as the natural conclusion to the day's toil. Little is drunk there but raw spirits, and the effect in a hot climate may be imagined. Neither was there any counteracting religious influence to check or control this disastrous state of things. There were neither churches nor priests within a hundred miles of their station, and only a rare visit now and then from some clergyman, on his way to perhaps a still more neglected flock, kept alive in the minds of the workmen the very knowledge of a God. Gwladys felt this privation terribly. No amount of meditation and prayer could make amends to her for the loss of the daily sacrifice, and the absence of loving words and saint-like counsels, which her lonely and desolate life so much required. And then there was no help from holy influences to touch her husband's heart—no bell ever summoned him from his sensual, material life, to think for a moment of heaven and hell. His days were spent in the saddle, when sufficiently sober to sit his horse; but week by week, as the heat became greater, and his powers of resistance less, the temptation of the grog-shop became more irresistible, and Gwladys had the horrible humiliation of seeing him brought home, day after day, by his own men, in a state which their delicacy of feeling tried to conceal from her, but to which it was impossible for her long to close her eyes.

So matters went on from bad to worse, till even Gwladys' brave spirit sank within her; while she momentarily expected the dismissal of her husband from the overseership he so unworthily filled, a dismissal which would have added pecuniary ruin to their other troubles.

In the midst of these increasing difficulties, anxieties, and sorrows, Gwladys became a mother. Untended, save by the wife of one of the stockmen, and deprived of almost all the comforts which her state so imperatively required, yet she passed through the fiery trial in safety, and neither she nor her boy suffered in any essential manner from the rough tending of their inexperienced yet kindly nurse. Gwladys herself had never expected to live through it, and had made all her little preparations accordingly. But when, the struggle over, she first heard the cry of her new-born child, a flood of joy and thankfulness rushed over her heart, and with it a passionate desire for life, which had now found an object to care for and to love. And when Lord William came in and saw her with her child in her arms, an expression of new and untold happiness lighting up her beautiful face, even his heart was melted, and stooping over the bed, he kissed both mother and babe with unwonted tenderness. During her convalescence, he was unusually quiet and well-behaved, rarely indulging in drink; so that a brighter future seemed in all senses to open on poor Gwladys, and she began to entertain hopes of a reformation of the father, through his love of the child. But she had not calculated on the force of evil habits once become inveterate, with the absence of any religious principles to influence or restrain. The momentary excitement of pleasure at the birth of his boy passed away, and with it his good resolutions. He was now scarcely ever sober, and no efforts on Gwladys' part availed to hide his state from the superintendent of the station. The fidelity of the labourers towards her—one and all of whom had some little tale to tell of her past kindness and thoughtfulness towards them—showed itself in a thousand delicate and kindly ways, and especially in their endeavours to keep things straight on the Run, which their master's neglect would soon have brought to utter ruin. In addition to the surliness he had before exhibited, he now became, at intervals, furiously violent; so much so, that Gwladys began to fear for her life, and wonder if madness were hereditary in his family, or if his state was merely the consequence of continual intoxication. His bodily health seemed to give way at the same time; he became fearfully emaciated, his clothes hanging about him as if made for another man, and his eyes acquiring that blood-shot, lack-lustre look, so characteristic of the habitual drunkard. His thirst was incessant, and with all Gwladys' watchfulness to keep the temptation out of his way, his rage, if his desire for brandy were not instantly gratified, made him resort to personal violence, both towards her and their child, so that she learned to dread his coming footsteps, and to deprive herself of the consolation of her baby, whom she entrusted to the care of their rough but faithful servant, too thankful that on herself alone should fall the cruel blow, which several times had followed the fearful oath, which generally ushered his return home.

And soon the end drew near. The paroxysms of delirium tremens became more frequent, to be succeeded by a depression and despair which were even more trying to witness, and perhaps to bear. At times he would reproach himself bitterly for his conduct to Gwladys, and ask her forgiveness in the most moving terms.

During one of these transient periods of penitence and compunction, he spoke to her of his own family—of his mother and sisters—and of his earnest wish that, when all was over, she should return to England with their boy, that he, at any rate, might have the advantages of an English education, and be brought up in his father's faith, and according to his rank and position in life. Gwladys promised all he wished, and strove to lead him to think of preparing for the change which she felt was inevitable. But the heart which had so long been closed to thoughts of God and the future, was even more hardened now. As he had lived so he died, without hope, without prayer, and so suddenly towards the last, that Gwladys, who had been nursing her child in the adjoining room, was only summoned in time to receive his last sigh, and catch the last agonising look with which his eyes, already partly dimmed with the glaze of death, followed her as she swiftly came and knelt by his bedside.

With a mixture of awe and terror, Gwladys knelt on, her lips unable to form a prayer. The thought that he was gone, thus unprepared, to meet his Judge; the agonising fear lest she should have neglected the means which she might have used to bring him to a better mind, paralysed her heart and brain. One only cry for mercy for him—for herself—burst from her ere she fainted by the corpse of him who had so cruelly blighted her young life. The rough farm servant, alarmed at her mistress's state, did her best by pouring water on her face, and chafing her hands and feet, to restore her inanimate form; and at last bethought her, with a woman's instinct, of fetching the baby and placing it in her arms. The sharp wail of the little boy effected what she had hoped, and Gwladys, opening her eyes, with a kind of shudder, clasped her child closer to her breast, and her pent-up misery found vent in a burst of tears.

CHAPTER IV.

*When the rich and noble suffer,
Then the fame is spread abroad;
When the poor and humble suffer
No man knoweth, only God!*
                                CHESTER.

WE pass over the events of the next few weeks. Gwladys, by the sale of the stock, found herself in a position to discharge the heavier portion of her husband's liabilities, and with the assistance of her first colonial friends, the Levins, returned to Sydney, and prepared to fulfil her husband's last wishes with regard to going to England, and introducing their child to his father's family. But first she wrote to his mother, not without some trepidation, we must confess, for nothing she had heard of that lady had tended to reassure her. But she thought it right to let her know the circumstances of her son's death, and of his wishes as regarded his boy; and having done so, she resolved to wait patiently for a reply. The Levins begged her to take up her residence with them during the remainder of her stay in the colony; and this kindness she accepted, on the condition that she was to be at liberty to earn her own living and that of her child by giving lessons in music, for which she was fully qualified, and which prevented what would otherwise have been, in her mind, a painful feeling of dependence on others.

After many months' delay, the answer arrived from the duchess. Mrs. Levin saw with pain the crimson colour mounting in Gwladys' face as she read the note and involuntarily crushed it in her hand.

They were alone that evening, and when the children were gone to bed, Mrs. Levin, gently drawing Gwladys towards her, whispered:

'What fresh trial has my poor child had to-day?'

With a burst of tears, Gwladys drew forth

the letter, which Mrs. Levin read with an indignation even exceeding her own:—

'Madam,—I have received a letter purporting to be from the wife of my late beloved son, Lord William de Tracey.

'As I was not aware he was married, you must allow me to doubt the fact until I have a better proof of it than your own assurance to that effect, and I should likewise require a baptismal certificate of the supposed child as an evidence of its legitimacy.

'FRANCES DE TRACEY,
'Duchess of Sandon.'

Mastering her anger, after a few moments, Mrs. Levin said calmly:

'This is a letter which my husband must answer and not you. Give me the necessary papers—both as regards your marriage and your child's birth. We will have them duly copied, attested, and sent to her. After all,' she added, 'it is perhaps not altogether unnatural and unreasonable that she should require proofs of a fact which seems to have taken her so entirely by surprise. But how is it possible that Lord William never mentioned you to his family?'

'He had quarrelled with them all,' replied Gwladys sadly, 'and had started for Australia to escape from his creditors, without letting even his mother know his whereabouts. Thus much he told me, but he was very reserved on this point. The only thing I gathered from his last words respecting them was, that he had one sister named Elizabeth, whom I should love, and "who would be a comfort to me," he said; which implied, I am afraid, that the others would not.'

'Well, you must not go to England till this matter has been cleared up, so we shall keep you a little longer,' said Mrs. Levin, smiling; 'and now go to bed and forget these hard words, dear Gwladys, or rather offer them up, as you know how. We will put it all straight for you.'

It may perhaps seem strange that Gwladys never once thought of returning with her child to the Mauritius; but a feeling of delicacy restrained her. Miserable as her married life had been, still Lord William had been her husband, and, after his fashion, he had loved her. Besides, he had left her a grave charge, the care of their boy; and the more she had found it impossible to feel towards him as a wife should, the more scrupulously did she fulfil every duty of her state. Poor as the substitute was for real love, it was all she could give, and she gave it honestly, conscientously—almost gladly. It seemed to soothe her to think that in this respect she had never broken her marriage vow, and in the care and nurture of her boy she had an abundant reward and consolation. For he was a most engaging child, gentle, obedient, and good, and though, in pursuance of her husband's wishes, brought up a Protestant, still she hoped that when old enough to judge for himself, the loving influence of the only parent he had ever known would induce him to follow in her steps.

And so the next year or two glided on calmly, if not happily. During that time many sought to win the heart of the gentle sad-looking widow, who had always a kind and charitable word for the sick or the sorrowful, and whose beauty had perhaps even acquired a greater charm in the crucible of trial. But Gwladys had never loved but once—all other affection of the like nature seemed to her a sacrilege; and so she went on her way, refusing to see what it would have given her pain to repulse, and under the shelter of her friend's roof was safe from the unwelcome attentions and the persecutions which the selfishness of men so often entails on women in her position.

No answer, in the meantime, had been received from her husband's relations, although Mr. Levin had taken care to ascertain that the needful papers had safely reached the duchess's hands. They were evidently determined to ignore her and her child, and that, for her boy's sake, Gwladys felt she must not allow. In one of the few conversations on pecuniary matters which she had had with her husband, he had told her of a small property left to him by an aunt who had been his godmother, and which was entailed on any son of his, although, in the event of her dying without issue, it was to go to his next brother. This estate would be a certain provision for her little Reginald, and she resolved to claim it at all personal pain or risk. Mr. Levin fully concurred with her in this view, and also in the duty which was incumbent upon her to assert her child's rights and position in England. So that, after mature deliberation, it was decided that she was to go to London and endeavour to arrange the matter amicably with her husband's family, failing which Mr. Levin gave her the address of a lawyer of unimpeachable honesty, into whose hands he advised her to place her case. The absence of all settlements at the time of her hurried marriage rendered some steps of this sort of paramount importance, as Gwladys had only her own earnings to depend upon, and they were utterly inadequate to meet the expenses of Eton, on which Lord William told Gwladys he had set his heart for his boy.

For some months she had, by extra lessons and by the sale of her drawings, in which she excelled, contrived to put by a certain sum to defray the cost of the voyage, and of her first arrival in England. Afterwards, she fondly hoped that her case was too clear to be doubtful, even should she not succeed (as most of her friends thought was certain) in winning her way with her new relations. Some wondered at her courage in thus facing the ocean and an untried future alone with her boy. But Gwladys' was not a nature to be deterred by difficulties. When once she was convinced a thing was right and a duty, she went simply forward, trusting in God, neglecting no human means to bring about a favourable issue, but leaving the result in His hands.

And so, one fine October morning, the last farewell having been said, and the last blessing given in the little church where she had daily sought for and obtained the strength suited to her need, Gwladys found herself on the deck of the fine steamer 'Hope,' bound for Point de Galle and the Overland Route; her little boy charmed (as all children are) with a change, and already having made friends with half the ship's company. To Gwladys' great delight, two or three missionary priests had likewise taken their passage in the same vessel, so that day after day, at early dawn, she had the untold comfort of the Holy Sacrifice.

She met with nothing but kindness and courtesy on board; from the bluff old captain who placed her by his side at every meal, and was never satisfied unless she would eat of everything he thought best, down to the little steward's boy, whom she had saved the first day from a serious scolding, and who vowed devotion to her from that moment, every one was considerate and kind, and did their utmost to beguile the tedium and suffering almost inevitable in a long voyage. As for her boy, he became a general favourite; his beauty, his spirit, together with his tender deference towards his mother, won all hearts, and Gwladys' only fear was lest he should be irretrievably spoiled by both passengers and crew.

The novelty of the arrival at Suez, the

beauty of Cairo, where they were detained two or three days, and the interests of Malta and Gibraltar, of which he had read in his childish books, and which were equally new to his mother as to himself, made the voyage one of unmixed enjoyment to the boy; so that it was with real regret that he first saw the white cliffs of the Needles, and was told that the following morning would see them at Southampton. To Gwladys, likewise, in spite of her brave heart, this arrival was a moment of great nervousness and anxiety. She knew nothing of England or of English customs and habits, and so, thinking that the address given her in London of the family mansion was sure to be the right one, and that she was equally certain of finding them at home, she took the first train after landing at Southampton, and about five o'clock in the evening found herself in due course at the door of a large house in Grosvenor Square. She was surprised at the apparently desolate look of the square, and at the closed shutters of almost every window, and waited with some impatience for an answer to the cabman's ring, which seemed unaccountably delayed. Presently the door, still fastened by the chain, was cautiously opened, and an old woman's head appeared, and asked her business. Gwladys inquired if this were not the house of the Duchess of Sandon? The charwoman replied in the negative: adding that the house had been sold a year ago, and that she was alone in charge. Gwladys then asked if she could tell her where the family were gone to? And the old woman, seeing that she was evidently a stranger to London and its ways, replied:

'Why, ma'am, begging your pardon, where can you be come from to expect to find any of the gentlefolks in town at this time of year? Except it be political gents, or lawyers, or such like, there ain't a soul in these fine squares, unless, may be, there's some one very sick come up to see the doctors.'

'I am just arrived from Australia,' said Gwladys, rather sadly, 'and don't know England or London ways; but perhaps you could tell me of some respectable hotel where I could go for the night, until I can find out the people I seek.'

The address was given, and in a few minutes Gwladys found herself installed in a small, stuffy, and not over clean room, with a spindle-legged mahogany table in the middle, a black horse-hair sofa, and a blowsy, disagreeable-looking chambermaid, who asked her, not over civilly, 'if she wanted one bedroom, or two?' There were certainly far better apartments in the house; but they had no idea of showing them to a 'party' who brought no servants, and who had already remonstrated at the exorbitant fare of the cabman. Gwladys dismissed her, saying that one room would do, and begging to have some tea for her boy, who, tired and sleepy, seemed very much inclined to cry.

After more than a quarter of an hour's delay, a slip-shod waiter brought her part of a stale loaf, some bad butter, and lukewarm water, and a bluish-looking liquid by way of milk.

'So much for London,' thought poor Gwladys, who felt rather disposed to follow the example of her boy; but, struggling against the discouraging aspect of everything around her, she coaxed the smoky fire into a blaze, made Reginald a little toast, and then, his tea finished, put him to bed, where he speedily forgot both his troubles and fatigue in sleep; while Gwladys remained awake, hour after hour, thinking with no small anxiety of what she should do next. In her perplexity it occurred to her that she had better go to the lawyer whose address Mr. Levin had given her, and be guided by his advice. And so, accordingly, the next morning, taking her boy with her, she started for the city.

It was a regular November day, foggy, drizzly, and wretched in the extreme in the fusty cab, smelling of damp straw, which conveyed them through what appeared to Gwladys an interminable succession of the same dingy, dirty streets, until they reached the parts of Holborn which had been mentioned to her as the address of the lawyer she sought. Dismissing her cab (for the experience of the previous day had taught her the additional expense of keeping it waiting), she entered the chambers, and, after some difficulty, found on one of the doors, up a steep flight of steps, the wished-for name. After ringing again and again, without any apparent result, a small boy, with the remains of what had once been a mutton-chop in a tray on his head, came sliding down the banisters, and landed opposite Gwladys, whom he examined with a species of eager curiosity, which amused, while it rather provoked her.

'Is there no one at home here?' she exclaimed to him, with something like impatience, as he remained dangling his legs across the stairs, and appeared indisposed to give her the least assistance.

'You may ring at that door till you're black in the face,' replied the boy, impudently enough; 'the old gentleman's away.'

'Away!' echoed Gwladys, with such an expression of genuine distress, that it touched the heart of a respectable elderly man who was just descending the stairs from an upper room, and at sight of whom, the imp of a boy disappeared into the lower regions.

'Can I be of any service to you, madam?' he asked with gentle courtesy, looking with interest at the fair young face in the widow's cap, with the fine boy whose hand she held.

'Yes, sir,' replied Gwladys simply, 'if you can tell me where Mr. Barlow is to be found, to whom I have a letter, which I am very anxious to present to-day if I can.'

'That, I fear, will be impossible,' replied he, 'for he is abroad. Trevelyan,' he suddenly called out, to a young lawyer who was passing them on the stairs, 'can you tell me where Barlow is just now?'

'At the Italian lakes, the lucky dog,' replied the young gentleman. 'I wish I had his chance, or his tin; catch me stopping here in such weather as this!'

'Do you know his address?' continued the older man.

'No—yes—I think I do,' answered Mr. Trevelyan, catching a glimpse of Gwladys' soft face. 'If you'll stop a moment, I'll go back to my room and look.'

Gwladys thanked both with gentle dignity; and, whilst waiting for the direction, asked her new friend if he could give her any clue to the whereabouts of the Duchess of Sandon.

The old lawyer eyed her with still greater interest, while he replied:

'Yes; she has changed her house, and is now in Belgrave Square.'

'Is that near here?' inquired Gwladys, timidly.

'Near here? good gracious, no!' exclaimed the old man, laughing. 'I should like to see the duchess's face if you were to put such a question to her. But have you never been in London before?'

'Never,' replied Gwladys, 'or in England either. I was born in the Mauritius, and only arrived yesterday from Australia.'

'Poor thing! poor thing!' murmured the old man, with genuine compassion; but at that moment Mr. Trevelyan reappeared with the direction, and Gwladys, with renewed thanks, bowing to them both, took her way downstairs with her boy, who already began to feel himself a great man, and 'mamma's protector.'

Calling a fresh cab, not less miserable than the last (When shall we get decent street vehicles in London for ladies, as in Paris Rome, or Vienna?), she told the man to drive to Belgrave Square. Again the same reply came to Gwladys' sinking heart.

'This was the duchess's house certainly, but the family were in Paris. Would be home perhaps in a fortnight, couldn't tell;' and again the door closed upon her. To go back to her uncomfortable hotel and *wait*—that seemed the only alternative, a bitter one to a nature so impatient and eager for action as Gwladys', and which pecuniary considerations rendered more painful and perplexing. On her way back she stopped to buy a book to amuse her boy in the gloomy inn sitting-room, and then sat down seriously to consider what was to be done. To write to Mr. Barlow and explain her circumstances and her need of his assistance was her first resolve, but she shrunk from any further correspondence with the duchess, preferring to trust to the effect which a personal interview might produce, combined with the presence of her boy, who bore a striking though refined likeness to his father, which she trusted might touch the duchess's heart. She was roused from these reflections by a joyful cry from Reginald, who, in the passage, had discovered a playmate and acquaintance of his on board ship, whose parents begged Gwladys' permission to keep him with them for the rest of the day, and take him with his little friend to see the Polytechnic. The fact of her being known to these people, who were rich, and above all the magic word of 'ladyship' which they naturally addressed to her, worked a sudden change in her treatment by the people of the house, the head of which came in person to apologise for the bad accommodation they had given her, and to beg of her to change her rooms. She inquired the price, and having already decided in her own mind that she would only remain there a few days longer, till she could look out for lodgings and employment, she chose, for her boy's sake, a more cheerful sitting-room, looking on the street instead of a blank wall, and then set herself quickly to work to write to Mr. Barlow.

Towards dusk, having posted her letter, she felt an irresistible longing to find herself once more in a Catholic church; and having asked the way of a poor woman selling oranges at a corner of the street, turned down a narrow passage, and found herself suddenly at the gate of a rather gloomy-looking building, into which you descended by a flight of dirty steps. Pushing open a heavy door at the bottom, however, Gwladys found herself suddenly in the midst of a great congregation of very poor people, in a spacious but almost subterranean church, in which the only remarkable feature was a large finely-carved white stone high altar, and a beautiful crucifix, the size of life, which formed the end as it were of one of the side aisles. From the altar steps, when she entered, a man was preaching, whose voice and manner at once arrested her attention. Rather above the middle height, with a pale and ascetic countenance, yet wonderfully lighted up with Christian love, he was speaking from his heart of divine charity, of its power, of its influence, of its great example, and of the individual care taken by Him for each one of us, however poor — however humble — however desolate: how the trials of each were meted out by a loving hand, and strength given to bear them all, if only the burden were cast at His feet, Who had died on the Cross to teach us that the law of suffering is the law of God's kingdom, and that in one way only could we follow Him. Gwladys listened and listened till the distress and perplexities of the day appeared as if lightened of half their care. Benediction followed, and then the congregation dispersed; but Gwladys remained kneeling before the crucifix absorbed in prayer till a gentle voice at her shoulder whispered to her that the church was about to be closed for the night, and Gwladys saw before her the priest whose words had had such an effect upon her that evening. A sudden thought flashed across her that he would be the best person to whom she could turn for advice in her present difficulties; and so, asking to speak to him, he at once conducted her through a small sacristy up a few stairs to a dingy little room, in which the only furniture consisted of a broken-down sofa, a rickety table, and two shabby chairs. Gwladys looked round with an expression of involuntary surprise, which was not lost on her host. He smiled, and said:

'I dare say you never before were in such a wretched room as this, but a Catholic priest in London must not be particular, and I like living in the midst of my poor people.'

Gwladys simply told her story, and asked him where she could find suitable lodgings and employment until her affairs could be in some way arranged. The good priest paused in evident perplexity. Gwladys was still so young for such a struggle with life! However, he saw how much she needed cheering, and so replied:

'I will inquire for you to-morrow, dear

madam, but in the meantime you must tell me what you can do, and in what way I can best find you work.'

'I can teach music and drawing,' replied Gwladys, 'and I can write and copy anything that may be given me; but I cannot do needlework well, I have never been used to it.'

'In this case it need not be a subject of regret,' replied Father St. Clair, 'for nothing is so miserably ill paid in London as sewing. But you must give me time to think over what you have told me, and to make some inquiries,' he continued, rising, as he saw Gwladys preparing to leave. 'If you will give me your address I will come to-morrow evening, and let you know the result. In the meantime, keep up your heart. I see you have a brave spirit, or you would not have come all alone from the Antipodes to this great Babel for your boy's sake! and you know where to take your troubles, as I saw this evening,' he added, still more kindly, as Gwladys warmly thanked him. 'But stay,' he added, as she was passing out of his poor doorway alone into the gas-lit streets, 'you do not know London; you must not go out alone at this time of night;' and so calling his housekeeper to attend her to the door of the hotel, he once more blessed her meekly bowed head, and returned to his room. But not at once to his usual work. Gwladys' visit had strangely moved him; and he continued striding up and down, giving vent occasionally out-loud to his thoughts:

'So young, so *bien-née* looking, so pretty, unfortunately,' he murmured. 'What on earth is to be done with her in this vile town? How save her from the annoyance to which she is sure to be exposed? It would never do for her to go out and give lessons; copying-work at home is the only thing I can think of for her—but even that is overstocked, like all the rest. And then that mother-in-law of hers. I misdoubt the poor child's success *there!* I have been told she is hard as the nethermost millstone. But God can turn all hearts to His will,' he added reverently; 'I must pray for her! that's all I can do to-night;'

and with that last reflection, he resolutely turned back to his desk, and set himself vigorously to make up for lost time.

And Gwladys, having safely reached her destination, and listened patiently to the eager and joyous description which Reginald gave her of his day's pleasures, laid her head on the pillow with a grateful trustful heart, and the shadow of a great peace fell upon her as she watched the even breathings of her beautiful sleeping child, and felt the fulfilment of the promise, 'Let their widows trust in Me.'

In a few days, through the indefatigable kindness of Father St. Clair, Gwladys was established in two tolerably tidy rooms, in a little street not far from the church, for which, however, a guinea a week was demanded, and with all her exertions she found it impossible to earn much more than that by her pen; so that she began to look with alarm at the inroads on her slender store which their daily food entailed. She was cheered, however, at this time by a very kind answer from Mr. Barlow, promising to return the following day and take her case in hand: and also on inquiring once more at the house in Belgrave Square, where opening shutters seemed to give indications of a change, to hear that 'the family' were to be in town for a fortnight the following Tuesday. It was on Sunday evening that this good news was brought to her, which she joyfully communicated to Father St. Clair. He was unwilling to damp her courage, but from his greater knowledge of the world conceived very grave doubts as to her reception by her husband's family, and endeavoured gently and delicately to prepare her for it.

'You have yet to learn how little heart there is in some of London's fine ladies,' he said to her one evening when Gwladys had been indulging in somewhat bright anticipations of the future. 'There is such a crust of worldliness and selfishness about them that all natural affections seem dead, or at least buried out of sight. And they are like cannibals—feeding on each other's reputations. O! the sins of the tongue for which those poor women will have to answer some day! I don't want to discourage you too much, Lady William,' he resumed, seeing Gwladys' face fall as he spoke, 'but I want you not to be too sanguine, and to be prepared for a long and hard struggle before you gain the place to which you are entitled in their affections.' How hard and hopeless this struggle would be poor Gwladys never dreamed; but before we arrive at this part of her history, we must give some account of the aristocratic family of which she so unwillingly, poor child, had become a member.

CHAPTER V.

La langue des femmes est une épée, et elles ne la laissent pas rouiller !

In a large and beautifully furnished room in Belgrave Square, and by a bright fire which a radiating grate threw in increased warmth on the occupiers of the arm-chairs round it, sat or rather lolled a young girl of nineteen or twenty, lazily playing with the silky ears of a little Chinese dog in her lap. Everything around her bespoke riches and luxury, from the priceless Sèvres on the mantelpiece and the rare chefs-d'œuvre of old masters on the walls, down to the soft Axminster carpet, on which the noiseless tread of the groom of the chambers was scarcely heard while carefully arranging the elegant writing-table or putting fresh water to the exquisite bouquets of hot-house flowers which were scattered here and there on the little etagères and whatnot tables with which the room was perhaps inconveniently crowded. The young lady herself—dressed in the last Paris fashion, her hair dyed gold colour, and turned off her face so as to give it as little shade as possible—was fair and good-looking, with a certain aristocratic air of good breeding impossible to define, but which was felt in every turn of the well-shaped head and every play of the little foot, encased in a velvet slipper, and which she was comfortably toasting before the cheerful fire. Yet, in spite of the high-bred look and delicate curl of the short upper lip, Mary de Tracey's face was not a pleasant one. There was a hardness in the eyes and in the lines of the mouth which chilled you without knowing exactly why, and no one would have gone to her in trouble or cared to claim her sympathy for a tale of sorrow or of wrong. Far different was the face of another girl in the same luxurious apartment, who was copying music at a table not far from her sister's chair. There was an undeniable family resemblance between them, but there the likeness ceased. A warm, loving, and tender spirit, unchilled by the worldliness around her, lit up her soft blue eyes, and gave an indefinable charm to her bright smile and genial manner. All strangers clung to Elizabeth de Tracey, and felt at home with her at once; while little children loved and clung to her, and the sick, and the poor and sad-hearted sheltered themselves beneath her gentle sympathising words and looks from the neglect or scorn of the 'fine ladies,' who had invented a new road of their own by which to get to heaven.

The door suddenly opened, and a merry guardsman cousin walked in, giving a warm kiss to Elizabeth, and a mock one from the tips of his fingers to Mary, while he exclaimed:

'What's in the wind to-day I should like to know? Her grace looks as black as thunder, and nearly bit my nose off for some innocent remark I made coming out of the breakfast-room; what have you two been doing to her? Bringing her in an unpayable bill from Palmire, Lady Mary? or aggravating her beyond bearing by talking of sisters of charity, Betsey?'

'Neither one nor the other, Sidney,' replied his eldest cousin; 'simply that the *wind is in the east*, and has been so for ever so many days, heaven knows why! Mamma delights in mysteries you know; and so, as for getting at the bottom of what's vexed her, unless she chooses to divulge it, *c'est autant de temps perdu.* Why, she came down upon me like anything only yesterday, for having said to old Baron Horser that we were going into Yorkshire for Christmas, a secret known to her grace's footman and stable boy, and milk boy and butcher boy to boot! and she blew me up again for talking of Constance's marriage, which has been in every paper this fortnight. But she has been worse since the post came in this morning; so I suppose we shall have a bonâ-fide eruption of the volcano before long,' continued the dutiful young lady, leaving her arm-chair to walk to the window.

'You won't get any comfort there,' said her cousin, laughing. 'Such a day of hopeless down-pour never was seen. Well, I shall go to the club. My delicate health won't stand family scenes, you know,' he added in a whisper, as the door again opened and the duchess came in quickly and sat down to her writing-table without exchanging a word with her daughters or nephew. Hereupon the latter began a series of pantomime behind her back, till Elizabeth rose gently to remonstrate with him.

'Very sorry, can't help it, my dear,' was the whispered answer, while he stole another kiss of the bright kind face.

'"It is He that has made us, and not we ourselves," isn't that what you say in church every day? now don't look more shocked! I'm a horrid heretic, I know, but I'm not so bad as I'm painted, after all,' he added out-loud, as he gained the door and made his escape, before his aunt was well aware of his intention.

A complete silence followed his exodus, only interrupted by the scratch of the duchess's pen, as she wrote nervously several pages in a clear pointed hand; and then ringing a silver hand-bell summoned the groom of the chambers.

'Take this note to Messrs. Brassey, or rather send it in a cab by one of the footmen immediately, so that it may reach them before the office closes; and Howard,' she continued, in a voice which she in vain endeavoured to steady, 'when that wo——, that lady comes, who was here yesterday, show her up here.' Evidently something was very much the matter to agitate in such a way the usually haughty, impassible, and beautiful duchess. For beautiful she undoubtedly was: with a high forehead, straight and delicately-cut features, a nose which sculptors had made their model, and the short upper lip of her noble race; with a figure which age had as yet left unimpaired, and a tread which an empress might envy: not one of her children could compare with her in these particulars, though Mary had inherited a large portion of her beauty of feature.

But for the *soul* in the face, you might look in vain. All idea of generosity was belied by the thin lips which met tightly over her white teeth, while her eyes had an expression of glittering hardness alternating with feline cruelty, which reminded one irresistibly of some wild animal. 'Had she ever been a tender loving child?' people often asked themselves when watching her walk through her crowded rooms, filled with the *élite* of London society, yet insensibly chilling all with whom she came in contact. Yes, she had once been as Elizabeth was, affectionate, kind, bright, and happy; but she had been deceived in her husband, deceived in her sons, disappointed in her expectations of domestic happiness, and so, having no religious principles wherewith to learn to accept and meet the storm when it burst upon her, she resolved to defy it, to meet scorn with scorn, and hatred with hatred, so that if she could not win love, she should at least inspire fear. Add to this, an intense worldliness, an overweening love of power, and an overwhelming pride of birth and station, and you have a fair picture of the woman before whom Gwladys was about for the first time to appear in the position of a daughter-in-law.

For a long time after the departure of the servant, the duchess was silent, nervously twisting in her fingers the pen she held, and unconsciously tearing the feathers off in strips. The girls watched her, one with hard surprise, the other with pain and anxiety, not knowing what was coming next. All of a sudden the clock struck twelve, and a little click at the drawing-room door gave notice that some one had rung the front door 'company's' bell. The duchess sprung to her feet visibly paler, and said in hard and measured accents: 'The lady who is coming upstairs is your sister-in-law, your poor brother William's widow. I have tried to forget her existence, for heaven knows who she is or where he picked her up. But those sort of people take no hints and have no delicacy, of course. So she has hunted us out in England, and, what is worse, has brought her boy. Unfortunately, there is no doubt of the truth of her story; he did marry her: and so to avoid an *esclandre*, we must try to get rid of her as quietly as we can.'

The words were scarcely out of her mouth when Howard noiselessly opened the door and announced Lady 'William de Tracey,' and Gwladys came in leading Reginald by the hand. So completely did her refined, ladylike and dignified appearance take the whole family by surprise, that the set speech the duchess had prepared for the occasion failed her, and she contented herself with a stately curtsey, closely imitated by Mary; while Elizabeth, colouring between surprise and pleasure, took her hand, and led her to the nearest chair.

'You are Lady Elizabeth,' said Gwladys, faintly smiling, 'are you not? Poor William told me you would be a kind sister to me. Reggie,' she continued, 'this is your Aunt Elizabeth, of whom poor papa was so fond. Go and give her a kiss.' The boy, who had looked strangely and rather defiantly at the proud lady who had received his mother so coldly, smiled at Elizabeth, and put up his

A cold Reception.

face to be kissed, while he glided his little hand into hers.

'How marvellously like!' was all that the poor girl could say between her joy at seeing her brother's child and her distress at the manner in which his mother had been received. An awkward silence followed. The duchess glanced at Reginald, and a dimness came over the hard look in her eyes, showing that in spite of herself she could not entirely stifle the voice of nature in the recollection of what his father was at the same age; but conquering the whisperings of her good angel, which urged her to clasp the little fellow to her breast, she coldly said: 'Lady William, may I ask what your motive and intentions were in coming to England?'

'I have come to fulfil my husband's dying request,' replied Gwladys, firmly, her spirit rising in spite of herself at the question. 'He wished that his boy should be made known to his family, and that he should likewise have the advantages of an Eton education. The night before his death he told me that a small estate left him by an aunt and godmother was entailed on his son, and would be amply sufficient for his education and maintenance. That estate I am come to claim on his behalf, and have already instructed my lawyer to communicate with your grace on the subject.'

'Which he has done,' replied the duchess; 'but I fear your expectations on that head will be doomed to disappointment. That little property was so heavily mortgaged by Lord William, in order to meet his liabilities before leaving England, that it does not bring in enough to pay its expenses. But that you will doubtless have explained to you by your own solicitor.'

Gwladys bowed in silence, for her heart was too full to speak. This, then, was the meeting on which she had reckoned for months, this the home which was to shelter herself and her boy! Not a word had been said of him or of his future prospects should this expected inheritance fail, and her knowledge of Lord William's extravagance rendered the duchess's version of the affair only too probable.

Strange that such a possibility never had

occurred to her before. Elizabeth, in the meantime, was on thorns to know how to show her some of the love with which her heart was running over, without offending her mother, when it occurred to her to propose to take the little fellow up to her room and show him her birds.

'Will you come, too, mamma?' said Reggie, eagerly; 'O! do come. She has promised to give me a book of papa's too,' he added, in an audible whisper, 'a book that he had when he was my age.'

Gwladys rose to follow, unmindful of the angry looks which passed between mother and daughter; and in a few minutes found herself in Elizabeth's room, a bright, cheery den, full of books and pictures, and pets of different kinds, which enchanted Reggie, who set himself instantly to examine and make friends with them all. No sooner was the door shut than Elizabeth, throwing her arms round Gwladys' neck, exclaimed:

'O, I'm so glad to have you at last to myself. You darling little sister; I may call you so, may I not? And think of my never knowing of your existence till half an hour ago. How is it that William never wrote and told us? Poor William,' she added, with a tender sadness of voice and manner, 'he was very wild, but he had a kind heart, and he always loved me, as I did him. Do tell me something about his last moments? we heard nothing but the fact of his death, and that was all.'

But Gwladys, who had been proof against the haughty looks and cold words of the duchess, could not stand the loving ways of her new-found sister, and after a fruitless effort at self-control, burst into a flood of tears.

'O! how sorry I am,' exclaimed poor Elizabeth, with genuine compunction at having been, as she thought, the cause of this unexpected outburst.

'Do forgive me! it was very stupid and thoughtless of me to have talked like that of your sorrow.'

'It is not that,' murmured poor Gwladys, striving to regain some outward composure, 'it was your kindness which upset me after—'

'Yes—yes—I know too well, my poor little

sister, what you mean,' replied Elizabeth, hastily interrupting her; 'but what can I do? Mamma and Mary are always like that, so hard and cold! It breaks my heart sometimes, but they won't listen to me, and I find the only way to keep peace in the house is to hold my tongue; they know very well what *I* think of their cruel speeches and bitter words! But you mustn't mind them, indeed you mustn't, but make me your real sister, you know. What do they call you—Gwladys? O! I like that name. It is that of the daughter of Sir David Gam, who married first a Vaughan and then a Herbert, and whose father was knighted at Agincourt. Well, then, Gwladys, you must begin at the beginning, and tell me where you first met William, and all about it,' she continued gaily; 'and you, my little man,' she added, 'if you have done looking at that box of treasures, here is the book I promised you, with papa's name written in it, you see, and which will amuse you whilst mamma and I are having a cosy chat.'

So establishing Reginald in one corner, and

having forced Gwladys into a cosy little armchair by the fire, while she sat on a stool close by, she drew her on to talk of the past. Gwladys spoke of her beautiful Mauritius home, and touched lightly enough on the episode of her marriage; but this was unperceived by Elizabeth, who became absorbed in her description of her Australian life, and the difficulties they had had to encounter on their first arrival there. How long they would have sat on no one can tell, when there came a knock at the door, and Howard's head answered Elizabeth's somewhat impatient 'Come in.'

'My lady, her grace, has sent me to say the carriage is at the door, and that she is waiting for you.'

'For *me!*' exclaimed Elizabeth, 'how very provoking; she never told me she was going out. Where is Lady Mary?'

'Going out riding, my lady,' replied Howard; 'the weather has cleared, and so both horses and carriage were ordered about half an hour ago.'

Muttering an expression of extreme annoyance, she told Howard to say she would be ready in a few minutes; and then turning to Gwladys, exclaimed:

'I see how it is; they were afraid of my being too long alone with you, and so ordered the carriage on purpose. Well, it can't be helped. We must try and meet to-morrow. Give me your address. If I can't come, at least I will write, and let you know the best time; but we must be cautious and prudent, you know, for fear of a row,' she added, while she rapidly tied on her bonnet and prepared to follow Gwladys and Reginald downstairs.

On coming into the drawing-room they found it empty; and while Elizabeth was showing her a miniature of Lord William as a child, which bore a striking resemblance to Reginald, the door again opened, and 'Lord Weston' was announced. Elizabeth shook hands with him as with an old acquaintance, and then introduced Gwladys as 'Lady William de Tracey, my poor brother's widow,' and the conversation became general. Lord Weston was instantly taken with Gwladys' face and manner, and having a great fondness for children, drew Reginald to him and began showing him a clever new puzzle on the table. Presently Elizabeth recollected something she had forgotten upstairs, and went to fetch it, leaving Gwladys and Lord Weston alone. The latter, with ready tact, drew her out to talk of her boy and a little of Lord William, whom he had known, and so they were sitting, in apparently intimate conversation, when the duchess reappeared. An angry spot rose to her cheek as she saw at a glance the favourable impression Gwladys had made. Lord Weston was a clever political *habitué* of her house, whom she found agreeable and useful on many occasions, and for him to take a fancy to one whom she had determined beforehand to dislike and avoid was as if he had gone over to the enemy's side. With the instinct which was habitual to him, Lord Weston instantly saw the mistake he had made, and as the duchess's interest was valuable to him at that moment in a political sense, he resolved at once to retrieve his error. Gliding away instantly from Gwladys' side, and going up to the duchess, whose hand he lightly pressed, he said in his softest accents:

'I began to fear that the faithful Howard had deceived me when he said you were at home this morning.'

'And you seem to have consoled yourself very readily,' replied the duchess, glancing at Gwladys as she spoke with ill-concealed irritation of voice and manner. 'Well, what news is there to-day?'

'Nothing pleasant,' replied Lord Weston. 'The leader of the Opposition made a most telling speech last night, and beat us on the clauses by a majority of five. But this evening will be the tug of war. Of course you are coming down to the House?'

'Yes,' replied the duchess, 'I want to hear young Gladstone speak, and they say he is to open the debate. They say he will be a great orator some day. But is there no other news?'

'None but the Italian,' replied Lord Weston, and that we have sent to the "Times" without any Cabinet reservation. But oh, by-the-bye, there's a grand bit of fresh scandal going about the town—that Lady Meriel Kingslake has jilted that good honest fellow Melville, who had paid her debts and loved her like a madman. She promised to ride with him at two, and then went and married Lord Marsden at eleven. It was all settled between them at the opera, it seems, the night before. Poor Melville is almost out of his mind; but his friends tell him he is well out of the scrape. I wish the young lady joy, for Marsden is over head and ears in debt, and she will soon agree with Marshal Saxe, I fancy!'

'What do you mean?' replied the duchess, laughing.

'Why, don't you know his famous lines?' replied Lord Weston.

> Malgré Rome et ses adhérents,
> Ne comptons que six sacrements :
> Vouloir qu'ils en soient davantage
>   N'est pas avoir le sens commun ;
> Car chacun sait que le mariage
>   Et pénitence n'en font qu'un.

'You are incorrigible,' answered the duchess;

and then they went on discussing in a low tone several other matters, with the design on the part of the duchess, in which she succeeded, of making Gwladys feel thoroughly *de trop* and uncomfortable. She had yet to learn that favourite method of tormenting adopted by London's *beau monde* towards those whom they are pleased to consider slightly their inferiors in birth and position—that marked ignoring of your existence in the room, which, among other people of less 'blue blood,' perhaps would be looked upon as the height of ill-breeding and impertinence. Luckily for her, at that moment, Elizabeth reappeared. Seeing at a glance how matters stood, and seizing her opportunity, she went up to the duchess, and said:

'As you are busy with Lord Weston, mamma, may I take Lady William home in the carriage, and then come back for you? I am afraid it is going to rain again.'

The duchess gave an ungracious assent; and Gwladys, advancing to take her leave, received an icy shake of two fingers of a cold hand,

and with a distant bow from Lord Weston, left the room.

Scarcely had the door closed when he exclaimed:

'Who is this wife of poor William's, duchess, who has dropped upon us from the clouds?'

'Rather, you should say, come up from another place,' replied the duchess, bitterly. '*Who* she is, Heaven only knows. I believe the only answer to be given is that of Princess Lastri the other day, "Ma chère, elle n'est pas née du tout." All I know is, that her name was Murray; that her father was a planter in the Mauritius, or something of that sort, who of course moved heaven and earth to catch a lord, and a duke's son to boot, for a son-in-law; and so poor William fell into the trap, I suppose, and was caught, and now she is come home on our hands with no money, and that boy besides!'

'Who seems, I must say, a very fine intelligent little fellow,' answered Lord Weston. 'My dear duchess, why not make some capital out of this *contretemps?* London's as dull as ditch-water. We want some new face.

Why not take up this new daughter-in-law, as you can't ignore her, it seems, and bring her out on your next Saturday night? *Elle ferait fureur*, with that soft face and those brown eyes of hers, and cut out Lady Palmerston's new beauty!'

'And my own daughters too,' replied the duchess, drily. 'No, thank you; I am not the least disposed to try that experiment. There's Elizabeth taken an absurd *engouement* for her already! I must try and buy her off, I suppose, by doing something for the boy. I believe one's sons were made to plague one alive or dead,' she added, with a *dépit* that made the wary and cunning little peer adroitly drop the subject and turn the conversation into another channel. For political parties ran high at that moment. The Government was very shaky, and votes were of the utmost importance. Greatly as Lord Weston had been pleased with Gwladys, he could not afford to sacrifice the favour of the duchess by pleading her cause: although in his heart he despised and detested the woman who felt no yearnings of pity for one thrown on the London world without money and without friends, and that one the widow of a son she had professed to love!

In the meantime, Gwladys was forgetting her momentary mortification in the loving words and ways of her newly-found sister, who deposited her safely in her humble lodgings, greatly to the disgust of the full-wigged coachman and the powdered six-foot footman, who considered their own dignity compromised by driving into so unaristocratic a quarter, and the latter of whom would scarcely take the trouble to let down the steps for a lady the door of whose house was opened by a not overclean maid-of-all-work. It was impossible for Gwladys not to feel the contrast between the house she had left and the dingy room to which she had returned; and as for Reginald, he did not hesitate to express his discontent.

'O! mamma, why can't we live in a nice house like Aunt Elizabeth, and not in this nasty dirty place?' the tears springing to his eyes as he spoke. 'You've every bit as great a right to be there as she has, and I can't bear being here!'

'Hush, my boy,' replied Gwladys, 'we must be content and thankful, you know, for whatever God gives us; don't you recollect what you said when Father St. Clair took you to see those poor people in the court the other day?'

Reginald coloured and was silent. He had been with the kind priest to a wretched room the week before, where they had found a boy of his own age in the last stage of a decline, lying on straw in one corner, with neither food nor firing, and yet bearing it all without a murmur. It had made a great impression upon him at the time, so that his mother's words made him thoroughly ashamed of his petulant speech. At this moment Mr. Barlow appeared, anxious to know the result of Gwladys' visit. For she had completely won his esteem and sympathy at their first meeting, and he felt he would leave no stone unturned to befriend one so lonely and so deserving of all the help he could give. She told him all simply and frankly, and asked his advice as to what she should do next.

'I suppose you must wait patiently, Lady William, and see what Lady Elizabeth's kind influence may bring about,' replied Mr. Barlow. 'On the whole, things have turned out better than I expected. You have evidently won one friend in the family, and perhaps she may be able to help you with the rest.'

He had scarcely done speaking when a note was brought from Lady Elizabeth. It ran as follows:—

'May we have Reginald for a few days with us? I think it might do good, and soften mamma towards you both. If you consent, send him by the bearer.'

Gwladys read the note, and unconsciously the tears came into her eyes. She never hesitated about giving Reggie this pleasure; but she felt an inward conviction that he would henceforth be separated from her more completely than she had ever before contemplated. She passed on the note to Mr. Barlow, and turning to her boy, said:

'Well, Reggie, Aunt Elizabeth wants you to go back to Belgrave Square and spend a few days with her—would you like it?'

Reggie's joyful face was a sufficient reply; but then, suddenly recollecting himself, he said hesitatingly:

'But won't you be very lonely, mamma?'

'Never mind, my darling,' was Gwladys' reply, 'I shall get used to that; and you know I must be very busy to-night, and work to make up for lost time.'

So saying, she kissed him, arranged his little wardrobe in a bag, which she gave to the servant, and Reggie trotted off joyfully to his grandmother's house. She watched him down the street, thinking, with a mother's pride, how beautiful he was—how unlike the other children who passed by; and then she came back to her little room, and, without heeding Mr. Barlow's presence, leaned her head on her hand and burst into tears. He did not interrupt her for some little time; he felt that the day's strain had been very great, and that a good cry would do her good. But after a bit, he left the fire-place where he had been standing, and drew a chair near hers, saying:

'Now, I want you, Lady William, to be a brave woman as you are, and look things fairly in the face. I think it is very probable—mind I don't say certain, but probable—that what has happened to-night may end in a proposal on the part of your husband's family to take your boy altogether, and educate him as his father wished. Are you prepared for this?'

Gwladys groaned.

'Not altogether, Mr. Barlow, surely! you don't mean that I should lose him altogether? No, I do not think I *could* stand that.'

'Perhaps it may not be proposed,' said Mr. Barlow, gently; 'but I want you to consider the thing as possible, and reflect on the manifest advantages which would accrue from such an arrangement to the boy himself. You do not think yourself at liberty, in accordance with your husband's expressed will and wish, to bring him up in your own faith; how then do you propose to educate him? The expenses of a boy of his rank at Eton are nearly

300*l.* a year. I have not yet received Messrs. Brassey's answer; but I know the duchess's clear head in business matters, and I am very much afraid that what she told you is true: that nothing can be expected from the estate entailed upon him till he comes of age. How would it be possible, then, for you to defray so heavy an outlay? Do not think me hard and unfeeling,' he continued earnestly, 'if I place the truth before you so plainly. I know that you would sacrifice anything for your boy's sake, and I want you calmly to think over this, which my knowledge of the duchess makes me believe will be the way she will propose to salve over her conscience with regard to her son's child; and not to risk, by a hasty refusal, the future prospects of one so dear to you.'

Long after the sound of Mr. Barlow's footsteps had died away down the quiet street, did Gwladys remain in the same position, looking into the fire and trying to conquer the rebellious feelings which the probable future before her had conjured up. To give up her boy! He, who had been the light of her eye, the joy of her heart; whose boyish tenderness had done so much to soften the terrible memories of her unhappy married life, to give him up to those who would teach him to look down upon and despise her for her birth, and, still more, for her faith. O! it was bitter indeed. And then when she thought of the loneliness without him, the way she should miss his bright face, and beautiful eye, and light step, and joyous, ringing laugh, a cold shudder came over her as if life would then indeed be to her a living death.

Yet, she never hesitated. She saw at a glance how probable Mr. Barlow's suggestion was: she thought over her interview with the duchess, and felt how little consideration or kindness she could expect from one so utterly dead to all natural feeling; and then she remembered her own small means, how impossible it was for her to supply her boy with even the ordinary comforts and pleasures of his age; and so she made up her mind that, if the proposal came, she would accept it,

The Decision taken.

crushing out of her heart every selfish feeling, and sacrificing her whole prospects of future happiness for his greater good.

There is in every generous decision, when once taken, a calm satisfaction which, for the time, almost compensates for the bitterness of the struggle which that decision has cost; and so Gwladys, having fairly conquered herself and taken her resolution, turned resolutely to the unfinished pile of copying before her, and determining to shut out all morbid thoughts, set herself vigorously to work to complete her daily task. No one who has not experienced the feeling can tell how pleasant it is to earn money for a given object. If her boy went to his grand relations, he would want many little things for which Gwladys' independent spirit did not like him to be indebted to strangers, and this thought gave quickness to her pen and redoubled the energy of her brave spirit, which was determined not to yield or give way to weariness till the whole was completed. And then fairly tired out, and smothering the gush of tears which would burst forth at the sight of the empty little bed beside her, she slept calmly and undisturbedly till the bell of the little church the following morning roused her to hasten to that presence which was her never-failing strength and consolation.

Mr. Barlow, when he returned the next day, was surprised to find with what calm Gwladys received the announcement that nothing could be expected for some years from the property her husband had left. He had seen the lawyers of the duchess, and represented to them in the strongest terms the injustice of leaving Gwladys and her child to struggle on without assistance from those who were bound to provide for them, hinting, moreover, at the scandal which such a proceeding would cause in the London world, a motive which he rightly thought would have more effect on her grace than any other. Messrs. Brassey had promised to see and confer with the duchess again upon the subject; but pending her decision, Mr. Barlow was anxious to know how Gwladys was getting on, and whether there was no way in which he or his wife could assist her. Gwladys was touched at his delicate kindness; but refused all invitations for the present, thinking it wiser to remain where she was till she was relieved from the anxious suspense about her boy. In the course of the day, she received from him the following characteristic note, scrawled in the ordinary school-boy fashion:—

'Dear Mamma,—I hope you are quite well. Aunt Elizabeth is very kind. I sleep in a little room next to hers, and she asked me to say my prayers to her as I do to you. Aunt Mary has got a dear little dog; but I don't like her as I do Aunt Elizabeth. Grandmamma kissed me yesterday when we were quite alone, and said I was very like papa. There is a very funny cousin here, who wears a great high thing on his head which they call a bearskin. He says he'll take me for a ride on his horse some day. O! mamma, I wish you were here too. Then it would be no end of jolly! We have much better things to eat here than at home, and such good jam for breakfast.

'Your loving boy,
'REGGIE.'

His first letter to her! Years after she found it—yellow with age and smeared with tears; but still dear to her in a way that none but mothers know. She felt brighter and happier after reading it, and gladly accepted Father St. Clair's proposal to take her to the Sisters of Charity, whose house was near at hand, and whose acquaintance she had already made in her daily walks to visit some of the sick and suffering poor in the courts round her home. For though Gwladys had little to give, she had eminently the power of soothing and of sympathising; and many a bed-ridden woman would listen for her quick and gentle step with feverish impatience, and count the hours till her welcome visit came round again. The kind mother superior, who knew her history, received her with open arms, showed her their *crèche* (for the little babies whose widowed mothers were compelled to go out to work for their daily bread), and their orphanage and day-schools, and all the rest of their works of love, which interested her so much that she forgot the time and the care which pressed so heavily upon her; so that it was with almost a joyous face that she met again Father St. Clair in the parlour, when, after an hour's absence, he returned to fetch her home. On entering the house, a fresh pleasure awaited her, in a note directed by Lady Elizabeth, and enclosing the first proof of a photograph of her boy, which, with thoughtful kindness, she had had taken the very first day he had come to Belgrave Square. It was strikingly like, and gave Gwladys even more delight than Elizabeth had reckoned. Another evening passed, and yet another, and still there was no answer from Messrs. Brassey, and no whisper of Reggie's return. At last, on the fourth day, a big packet was brought to her, which turned out to be the long expected reply from the lawyer. It was, of course, a carefully-worded and formal epistle, written by desire of the duchess, setting forth the embarrassed state of Lord William's property in the strongest terms, and winding up (as Mr. Barlow had expected) with a formal proposal to undertake the care and education of his son, on condition that he should be entirely given up into the hands of the duchess, and that Gwladys henceforth should relinquish all authority over, or interference with him, in any manner whatsoever.

This was even worse than poor Gwladys had anticipated, and she felt she must take advice before sending a reply. She wrote, therefore, to beg both Mr. Barlow and Father St. Clair to come to her the following morning. But Father St. Clair was out of town, detained by a dying bed, so that Mr. Barlow alone replied to her summons, and Gwladys, without a word, laid the letter before him. The good old lawyer read the letter in silence; but when he came to the last paragraph, a sudden dimness came over his eyes, causing him suddenly to take off his spectacles to wipe them, and vigorously blow his nose. Gwladys, watching his face, felt nevertheless that her sentence had been pronounced, and at last, with a voice which she in vain endeavoured to steady, said:

'I see you think there is but one course for me to take. But could there not be some stipulation made about my seeing him sometimes?'

'Surely, surely, Lady William,' replied the lawyer eagerly. 'We will take care to introduce a clause about that in the answer. Heaven help that woman, when her hour shall come to need mercy! Well, well, we must make the best of it. Give me some paper, and we will concoct a reply,' he continued; 'but we must be very cautious, and have everything clearly put down in black and white with such people as these.'

So saying, Mr. Barlow set to work, and in a short time produced a letter, which he read out loud to her; and Gwladys having approved of its contents, copied and despatched it to Messrs. Brassey's. Mr. Barlow then took his leave, contenting himself with a hearty shake of the hand she held out to him, and feeling that at that moment she could not bear even the faintest word of kindness or sympathy. And Gwladys! She remained where he had left her for a long while, leaning her head against the chimney-piece, while bitter thoughts chased one another through her mind. The deed was done, the sacrifice made. Did she wish it recalled? No. If the whole thing were to come over again, she felt she should have done the same; and yet it was not in human nature not to feel it bitterly, almost overpoweringly. To calm herself a little, she again sat down, and drawing her writing materials close to her, began a letter to Lady Elizabeth. It ran as follows:—

'I have complied with the duchess's wish, and given up my boy into her hands; stipulating, however, that I shall see him from time to time. By the love of God, by the love you bore to poor William, I conjure you to watch over him as I would have done; to train him up in the fear of God; to keep alive in his heart feelings of love and respect for me, his mother, and for my Church, which is dearer to me than life itself. You know I am a Catholic; and though, in pursuance with your brother's wish, and to soothe his dying moments, I promised that Reginald should be brought up in his father's faith, still it would be very bitter for me were he to learn to despise and dislike his mother's religion in the way which, I am told, is general among English Protestants. I implore you, therefore, to guard him, if you can, from this evil, and not to let him forget me. I am told you are going into the country in a few days. I *must* see Reggie first, to take leave of him. Tell me if you will send him here, or if I shall come to Belgrave Square. God bless you, dearest Elizabeth. Kiss my boy for me.

'GWLADYS DE TRACEY.'

Elizabeth received this note at luncheon, in the midst of a large and merry party; but her cousin Sidney, who was watching her, saw her colour rise as she read it, and the convulsive effort with which she swallowed down her tears, drank a glass of water hastily, and then went on mechanically joining in the conversation round her, while her mind was evidently far away. The luncheon over, and the ladies having taken their leave, Elizabeth walked slowly and dreamily into her little sitting-room, whither she was followed by Sidney.

'Now, what is the matter, Betsey?' he said tenderly and earnestly, dropping altogether the bantering way which he generally assumed, and which concealed a great deal of deep and honest feeling. 'What are the contents of that note which changed your face so at luncheon? I was terribly afraid you would have burst out crying outright.'

Elizabeth handed him Gwladys' note; his face grew longer as he read it, while he gave a long low whistle of dissatisfaction at the end.

'The worst of it is,' continued poor Elizabeth, 'that I knew nothing of this cruel scheme. Mamma seemed kinder to Reggie, and I was in hopes every day that she would ask Gwladys here too, and was only waiting for an opportunity to suggest it. And now, I see how it is. She is determined to wash her hands of her altogether, and to quiet her conscience, I suppose, by adopting the boy. It is too hard upon her. And if you knew how charming and pretty she is, Sidney, you would be still more surprised! Mamma will have it that she is of a low origin; but it is impossible to see her and to believe that. Even Lord Weston was struck with her here the other day, and is always asking me after her when he thinks mamma is not listening. But now, about her seeing Reggie, how is it to be managed? It is quite true that we leave London next week, and it would be too cruel not to let her even wish him good-bye.'

'I will take him myself this afternoon, if you like,' replied her cousin. 'I had promised him a walk and to get him a football, and so that will be a good pretext, and we need not say anything about Lady William up there,' he added, pointing to the drawing-room. 'Besides, I should like to see this *rara avis* of a cousin of mine, about whom you are always raving. I am sure I shall like her if she has brought up that boy, who is a thorough little gentleman in all his ways. But it's unlucky she's a Catholic, isn't it? *That* won't help her with her grace.'

'I am afraid in one sense it will help to justify all that she may do against her,' replied Elizabeth. 'If this story gets wind, and people begin to cry out against her treatment of poor William's widow, it will be quite enough to give as a reason the danger there would be of Reggie's imbibing her " idolatrous faith," and half the world will applaud her wisdom and "motherly foresight," and speak in terms of contemptuous pity of Gwladys as having deserved the separation. Little she knows the prejudice in England on this head, and how far it goes beyond her fears. Keep Reggie from sharing in it? How is that possible when he goes to school, where every class-book is filled with Protestant venom, and every fact is distorted to suit the taste of its Protestant author and Protestant reader?'

'Why, my dear Betsey, one would think you

were a Catholic yourself,' exclaimed her cousin in some surprise.

'I'm not a Catholic,' retorted Elizabeth, 'though I sometimes wish I were when I contrast their charity with our incessant backbiting and *mauvaises langues*. But I hate injustice and wrong, and the narrow-minded bigoted views of people who imagine that the established religion of this little island is the only way to heaven, when more than two-thirds of the Christians in the world are of a different faith. But now, if you will really be so kind as to take Reggie, I will go and call him before it gets too late; and you will leave him with her a good long time, won't you,' she added, giving her cousin a loving kiss as she rose. He nodded assent, and in a few moments Elizabeth reappeared, leading Reggie, in triumphant possession of a new stick which Lord Weston had brought him that morning, and in high spirits at the prospect of Miller's shop and innumerable footballs to choose from, which at that moment appeared to him the acme of human felicity.

Captain de Tracey encouraged him to chatter on about his mother and his former life till the wished-for shop was reached, and the much-coveted treasure secured. After which he said to his little companion: 'Now, wouldn't you like to show that nice big ball to mamma? I am going down to my club, and could leave you at her house for a little bit, and pick you up on my return.'

A bound of joy and an endeavour to kiss his thanks in the middle of the street was Reggie's reply, and Captain de Tracey could hardly keep pace with the little fellow's eager steps as he ran rather than walked to the well-known door.

Gwladys was, as usual, alone when they came in; but the atmosphere of refinement around her, which the poor furniture of the room could not destroy, and the taste with which the little things belonging to her were arranged on the table beside her, made Captain de Tracey at once understand what Elizabeth had said of her gentle birth and breeding.

Reginald threw himself into her lap, embracing her boisterously, and then, his good

The Real Cousin.

manners returning, introduced his companion as 'the cousin who had given him the football,' which he instantly and joyfully displayed. Gwladys rose with gentle dignity and with the heightened colour which the pleasure of seeing her boy once more had brought into her cheek, gave a chair to her visitor, and begged him to sit down.

'I come as a messenger from Elizabeth, Lady William, and in answer to your note,' said Captain de Tracey, with marked deference and yet great kindness of manner. 'I need not tell you that she was unaware of the fact it contained, and which has pained her very much,' he continued, with much feeling. 'But now, I am not going to stay and bother you when you are dying to be alone with your boy. I will go on and do my business, and call for him again on my way to dinner. Will that do, Reggie?' he said, smiling to the boy, as he rose to take his leave. 'You must explain to mamma that I am a *real* cousin you know, and that she must consider me as such,' he added, as he walked quickly downstairs.

Gwladys had not ears enough to content her boy, who went on talking, as the old nurses say, 'twenty to the dozen,' about the charms of his new home, of the pony he was promised when he got to Manby Castle, and of the Scotch terrier which 'he rather hoped' cousin Sidney was going to give him when he went into the country. Already Gwladys felt with pain that his little life was separated from hers; and yet she rejoiced unselfishly in the many pleasures which the kindness of his relations was heaping upon him. Feeling that perhaps this was the last time she might be able to see him comfortably and alone, she led him on by degrees into a solemn mood, and without attempting to preach to him, contrived to slip in a few words which she hoped he would remember when she was no longer by his side.

'You are going into a new home, my darling,' she said to him, when he had comfortably established himself in her lap, with his curly head lying on her arm and his big eyes fixed on her face; 'and in that home you will have many nice things; but you mustn't expect they will be all pleasant. And after Christmas you will probably go to school and be thrown with other boys and learn much that I would give all the world you should never know. Now, I want you to promise me two things—never to pass a day without saying your prayers, and always to try and keep in mind that *God sees you*. This last thought, if you will only try and remember it, will keep you from all evil. Will you try and think of these two things for mamma's sake?'

'I will, mamma,' replied Reggie, gravely, for his mother spoke with a tone of deep feeling which she rarely showed to him, and it made an impression which subsequent years never altogether effaced.

'One thing more, my darling,' continued Gwladys, drawing the little head still closer to her. 'When you are tempted to do wrong, to act selfishly, to say passionate angry words, as you do sometimes, remember what I have so often told you—how you wound and grieve not only me, but Him who had so loved you as to die for you. Will you recollect this?'

Reggie eagerly promised, and then Gwladys, fearful of wearying him, or destroying the good impression her few earnest words had produced, led him on to talk again of the new and bright life which was opening before him. Five o'clock came, and she despatched the little maid to get them a plum cake and some marmalade, so that Reggie's recollection of his last tea with her (O! how she choked at the thought!) might be a pleasant one. And so they ate and talked, and the time was all too short to Gwladys' yearning heart when the door again opened to admit Captain de Tracey.

'I am afraid I am rather late,' he said, in a hurried tone; 'but I thought you would like to have this little man till the last moment. Come Reggie!' he exclaimed, 'get your hat; I have brought my cab, in which we shall soon spin home and so avoid a scolding from her grace for keeping her waiting for dinner. I will try and bring him again,' he continued, in an undertone, to Gwladys, whose lips quivered in her effort to wish her boy 'good-bye' calmly. 'Recollect you have *two* friends at court now instead of one.' And so, hastily shaking hands with her, and listening with an unusual choke in his throat to Gwladys' fervent 'God bless you, my boy,' he dragged the little fellow downstairs and into his cab, the novelty of which, as he expected, diverted his mind from the momentary sorrow which parting with his mother had caused.

And rarely indeed did his boyish footsteps again gladden his mother's heart—rarely did she see him till laid low by sickness and unconscious of her presence! But we are anticipating, and must resume the thread of her sad story.

CHAPTER VI.

> All was ended now: the hope and the fear and the sorrow;
> All the aching of hearts, the restless unsatisfied longing;
> All the dull deep pain and constant anguish of patience,
> And, as she pressed once more the lifeless head to her bosom,
> Meekly she bowed her own, and murmured: 'Father, I thank Thee.'
> LONGFELLOW.

As long as there was a motive for exertion and her boy to work for, Gwladys had kept up bravely to her daily labour, and the accuracy of her copying and beauty of her handwriting had already secured her increased employment, through Mr. Barlow's kind interest in her behalf. But, the mainspring broken, she found it impossible to persevere. What was the use of toiling for hours for bread which choked her as she swallowed it *alone* in that dismal lodging? Father St. Clair had anticipated this state of things, and had been making inquiries among his friends for some situation as companion, which would afford her a certain maintenance, and perhaps the distraction of travel to wean her from brooding on a sorrow which had become inevitable. For the duchess, without any previous warning of her intentions, started suddenly for Manby Castle, the very day after Captain Tracey's first visit to Gwladys, carrying Reginald off with her, on the plea that the country would be better for his health, but in reality to circumvent the plans which she knew were forming by Elizabeth and her nephew to bring about a fresh meeting between Gwladys and her boy in Belgrave Square. A broken-hearted letter from Elizabeth on the eve of starting was brought to Gwladys by Captain de Tracey the following day, and if he had been interested in her the first time, he was inexpressibly touched the second, at the look of hopeless sorrow and yet resignation with which his sad news was received. He promised to keep her constantly informed of her boy's health, and of the course of education proposed for him, if, as he feared was but too probable, Elizabeth were comfortably established in Devonshire, fulfilling her daily round of not unpleasant duties with a loving gentle spirit which speedily endeared her to Mrs. Wilmot's heart, who learned to love her as her own child. Two years were passed in this quiet and uneventful manner. During that time, Captain de Tracey, faithful to his promise, had regularly kept her informed about her boy, and on two or three occasions Lady Elizabeth had enclosed letters in his, giving her many of those details for which her heart so yearned. She had likewise seen him twice, going up to London with Mrs. Wilmot, and on one joyful occasion having him with her for the whole day. He had been placed at a good school at Brighton, preparatory to Eton, to which he was to go the following year. Gwladys found him much grown and improved, and when the shyness inseparable from so long a separation from her had worn off, she was rejoiced to find him as loving and tender towards her as ever. One event, however, filled her with anxiety on his account, and that was Lady Elizabeth's marriage. She knew how he would miss during his holidays that steady, firm, yet gentle influence which his aunt had always exercised over him, and by which she had endeavoured, as far as possible, to supply his mother's place. For his grandmamma had not succeeded in winning a place in his affections—he feared, avoided, and often deceived her: and she, her momentary interest in him passed, was simply as indifferent to his existence as she was to that of every one else about her home who did not thwart her plans or interfere with her selfish or worldly ends. However, Elizabeth promised that a portion at any rate of his holidays should be passed with her, and with that assurance poor Gwladys was fain to rest content.

Another year passed, and Mrs. Wilmot, wishing to give Gwladys some change of thought and scene, proposed a tour in Scotland, on which occasion they visited all the beautiful country from the Pass of Dunkeld to Inverness, and again the still wilder mountain scenery of Ross-shire and the western coast of Sutherlandshire. They were returning by slow journeys to Edinburgh, when, on arriving at Greenock from the Crinan Canal, a telegram was put into her hand. Gwladys tore it open with changing colour. It was from Captain de Tracey, and dated the day before.

'Reginald is ill with fever at Eton; come at once. I have sent a duplicate of this to Edinburgh.'

'You must start instantly, dear Lady William,' exclaimed Mrs. Wilmot, when she had read the sad missive in Gwladys' trembling hand. 'Never mind me. My maid will do all I want. Let us find out the time of the night trains to London,' she continued, ringing the bell as she spoke. The waiter brought the Bradshaw; the express would start in an hour from Glasgow—so without losing a moment Gwladys set off, thankful for the necessity for action, which was more endurable than sitting down to wait, and endeavouring as far as she could to gleam some hope from the wording of the telegram. The absence of the words 'very' or 'dangerously' could not do away with the effect of the concluding *come at once.* Had he only been slightly ill, she felt she should not have been summoned so urgently. Neither would Captain de Tracey have taken the trouble to send two telegrams instead of one.

She got into the express in a sort of dull dream of pain, drinking with difficulty the glass of wine which Mrs. Wilmot forced upon her at starting, and repeating mechanically the words, 'Come at once,' which seemed to be graven into her heart and brain. And then the date—the day before. What might not have happened in those intervening twenty-four hours? Gwladys clasped her hands and prayed as she had never prayed before—not for his life, but for submission to God's will, whatever that might be. And so the weary night wore on, and the cold dawn broke, and station after station was passed with frightful rapidity, and yet all too slow for poor Gwladys' anxious heart. And then London was reached, and she called a Hansom and rushed from Euston Square to the Great Western, and there found a train just starting for Windsor.

The nearer she got to her destination the more fearful and agonising was the suspense. No flies were waiting at that early hour at the Windsor station, but leaving her bag with the porter, she flew rather than walked down the hill and over the bridge till she reached the door of the tutor's house, where her boy lay. There was no sanatorium in those days for such cases, and she knew that the care bestowed upon them was not great; still she hoped, and with an effort convulsively rang the bell, which was answered by Captain de Tracey himself. Gwladys looked up in his face, but her lips refused to form the question.

'He is alive!' said he, with a voice meant to be reassuring, but at the first tone of which all hope died out of Gwladys' heart.

'Alive! O, my God! is that all?' she murmured, and would have fallen had not Captain de Tracey caught her at the moment. Drawing her into an adjoining room, and hastily pouring her out a cup of tea, which stood on the table, he said to her tenderly:

'Now, Lady William, Gwladys—let me call

you so! You must be very calm and quiet while I tell you all about this sad affair. Reggie only sickened three days ago, and I heard of it quite by chance, through the father of another boy who was ill of the same fever. I came down directly to see what was the matter, and to take care that he had the best doctor, and all that. You could not have done more if you had been here yourself. Then he got worse, and I telegraphed for you. You got my telegrams?'

'Last night, on arriving at Greenock,' said Gwladys, faintly.

'And have travelled ever since, I see,' said Captain de Tracey, sympathisingly. 'Well, yesterday evening he became delirious, and has been so ever since; but the doctors say he may rally again, and become conscious. So you must not despair. Now, you must have some breakfast before you go up to his room. You must,' he continued, as Gwladys was persisting in her refusal. 'You have taken nothing all night, I'll venture to say; and recollect you will want all your strength for him,' he added, guessing that this thought might have more effect on her than any other. And he was right—for Gwladys forced herself to drink the tea and to swallow a few mouthfuls before she followed him up to the bedside of her darling. Yes, there he lay. More beautiful than ever in the fever—with his large eyes glaring wildly here and there—muttering incoherently about Castle Manby and his dog one moment—about his lessons and his boat the next—but ever and anon, bursting out with:

'O! why don't you take me home? Why mayn't I go to mamma? Let me go to mamma!'

'I am here, my darling! my own Reggie!' exclaimed Gwladys, throwing off her bonnet, and encircling him in her loving arms. A faint attempt at recognition, and then a relapse into unconsciousness, and the ever-repeated cry of 'Let me go to mamma,' was all that came to soothe her breaking heart. But in the midst of it all a kind of joy shot through her. He loved *her* best! However much his relations had tried to estrange him from her, *she* was the one to whom he turned in sickness and in pain, and the comfort of this was unspeakable. Through all that day and all the succeeding night and following day the delirium continued. The doctors came in at intervals, and prescribed something fresh from time to time, and Captain de Tracey brought her food and wine, and occasionally helped her when the paroxysms of fever made him violent and he was with difficulty kept in bed. But during all those hours Gwladys remained at her post, bathing his head and hands, and trying in every way to soothe and calm him. At last, towards the evening of the third day, a change came. The wild look in his eyes passed away, and for the first time he whispered in low faint accents, 'Darling mamma.' It was almost too much for Gwladys' bursting heart, but she felt how important it was to keep him from the slightest excitement or emotion in his fearfully weak state, and so only gently bent down her cheek to his and whispered:

'Are you better, my child?'

'Yes, much better, mamma, only so tired,'

said the poor little fellow, closing his eyes as if to sleep.

Captain de Tracey hastily ran for the doctor, who quietly said to him:

'The crisis is come. Now, all will depend on our being able to keep up his strength. With such a nurse as that mother of his, I do not despair; but still I fear there is very little hope.'

Coming into the room, he administered a strong cordial; and then, leaving minute directions with Gwladys as to what was to be done in the next few hours, the doctor and Captain de Tracey left her with her boy.

'Well, if he dies, she may take this comfort to herself,' said the doctor, when they were well out of hearing, 'that that boy of hers dies as pure as my little baby in the cradle upstairs; and that is more than can be said of most of these Eton fellows,' he continued, as he left Captain de Tracey to attend to his other patients.

'That's what comes of having a mother like that to pray for one,' said the young guardsman to himself, as he sadly thought of his own neglected boyhood, which had brought forth, with all his good qualities, a plentiful crop of weeds. 'I am terribly afraid, however, that that poor little fellow won't pull through; and then *how* is she to bear it?' he said out loud, as if the thought were almost intolerable to him.

He returned to the sick room, and watched through the half opened door her gentle, calm ministrations towards her boy; how, with light hand and noiseless step she hovered round his bed; or else breathlessly watched, without moving, the short moments of sleep which she flattered herself would recruit his failing strength, with the never-wearying patience, the tender devotion, which anticipated his slightest want; and as he watched all this, he groaned inwardly at the conviction that it was all in vain —that the boy would die.

And it was even so.

The morning found him conscious indeed, but fast sinking : the doctor came, and shook his head, while he glanced at Gwladys, who needed no words from him to tell her that all hope was gone.

But the very extent of her misery gave her courage. She asked the doctor and Captain de Tracey to leave her alone for a few moments with her boy: and then taking advantage of the short half-hour of unusual clearness of mind which often precedes death, she calmly told him the truth, and how God was about to call him home. She asked him to make an act of hearty contrition for the faults of his life past, to forgive freely all who had offended him, and to ask for mercy from Him who had died on the Cross that he might live for ever.

Reginald heartily joined in the simple prayer she put up for him in this sense, enumerating the little faults of his boyhood one by one, and humbly asking pardon for them. And then a great peace seemed to fall upon him, and also a great joy. 'Mamma, I am so happy,' he whispered. 'Our Lord is so good to me; there is nothing to suffer.'

He threw his arms round her neck and gave

her one long passionate kiss. 'Say once more "God bless you," darling mamma,' he murmured. She did so. They were his last words. Gwladys called back the doctor and Captain de Tracey with a calmness which surprised them both. But her agony was far too deep for tears. There was something too sacred in the stillness and peace round the dying boy for any outward expression of grief.

The three watchers stood silently round the bed, Gwladys lifting him up in her arms to help his ever-shortening breath, the doctor moistening his lips from time to time with wine and water; and then his little head fell back heavily on his mother's arm, and with one long deep sigh, his pure and innocent spirit returned to his Father who is in heaven.

Gwladys softly closed the beautiful eyes, smoothed the rich clustering hair off his temples, and laid him down; then she sat on the bed looking at him, and slowly and deliberately made the sign of the cross on his forehead. Captain de Tracey, awed and touched at her supernatural calmness, drew near to persuade her to come away with him, but she motioned him gently aside and said, 'Please leave me here alone a little while; I will come by-and-bye.'

He did not dare contradict her then, but slowly and sorrowfully withdrew with the doctor, whose eyes were running over at the sight they had just witnessed, although so hardened in a general way to scenes of death and sorrow.

'I shall never forget that, never!' he exclaimed at last, while Captain de Tracey sat sobbing like a child at the foot of the stairs.

'And you don't know half the misery of it, doctor,' he groaned out in the midst of his tears; 'the confounded pride of that noble woman's relations, or rather her husband's, virtually separated her from her child, and she has scarcely seen him these last three years! Thank God! I took care she should be with him at the last anyhow,' he continued; 'no one now can deprive either of them of that consolation.'

Announcement to the Duchess.

Mastering his emotion with difficulty, Captain de Tracey sat down to write a formal letter announcing the fact of the death to the duchess, whom he felt it would interest less than that of her lapdog, and then wrote, out of the fulness of his heart, to his cousin Elizabeth, telling her every particular, and speaking in the most enthusiastic terms of Gwladys' conduct throughout those terrible days and nights of anxious watching.

'She is one of whom it may be truly said "the world is not worthy,"' was his concluding sentence. 'I hope you will invite her to stay with you a little while when the funeral is over, as I dread the effect of a reaction when all cause for exertion is past.'

In his letter to the duchess he begged to know her wishes regarding the funeral, and added the following postcript :—

'If you wish it to be at Manby, I shall come down with Lady William, who has nursed her boy to the last, with a tenderness and a devotion of which few women would be capable.'

Having finished these necessary letters, and given the last sad directions preparatory to the removal of the body, he returned to Gwladys, whom he found at the foot of the bed, absorbed in prayer.

The whole aspect of the room was changed; no hand but hers had laid out that much-loved form.

He lay in his little graveclothes, his hands clasped in prayer; and on his breast were some white roses, which she had gathered at the open window and had gently laid there.

Captain de Tracey knelt too, and softly kissed the cold marble-white forehead: after which, turning to Gwladys, he whispered, 'For God's sake, for Elizabeth's sake, come now to take some rest. You have done all you can now. I will return here and watch while you sleep. He shall not be left.'

Gwladys rose mechanically, and suffered him to lead her into the adjoining room, where a bed and a cup of hot tea had been prepared by his thoughtful care.

She was too much spent with misery to

speak, but she thanked him by an earnest pressure of the hand, while he tenderly and almost reverently, bending down his lips to hers, kissed it and withdrew.

She drank the tea, and undressed and laid down; yes, it was quite true what he had said, 'she had done *all* now!' And with a sob of something like despair, and a heart-weariness even greater than physical fatigue, her head fell back on the pillow, and she slept the sleep of utter exhaustion for some hours.

It was dark when she woke. O! the misery of that waking, when, bit by bit, the whole frightful reality came upon her, and she felt herself for the first time utterly alone in the world. And then at last her tears burst forth, uncontrollably, passionately, with bitter cries for 'her boy, her darling boy.' The tender watcher by her bedside let her cry on for some time without giving any sign of her presence. But at last, thinking her poor overcharged heart had been sufficiently relieved, a loving hand pressed hers, and a gentle voice repeated her name. Gwladys looked up. 'Elizabeth!'

she exclaimed, and once more, as on that day in Belgrave Square, which seemed so long ago, the sisterly arms were thrown round her, and the violence of her grief was soothed by heartfelt love and sympathy. Elizabeth had started off the moment she had received Captain de Tracey's letter; and being in London, an hour sufficed to bring her to the house of mourning. She had heard all particulars of poor little Reggie's illness and death, and of Gwladys' touching calmness and heroism to the end, and her husband had gladly spared her for a few days to enable her to remain till after the funeral, and made her promise, if possible, to bring back Gwladys with her afterwards to their quiet country home. There was a struggle in the duchess's mind between her dislike at the idea of having her daughter-in-law under her roof and her still stronger objection that a scion of their house should be buried in a strange churchyard in a nameless grave. But the latter feeling prevailed, and an answer came to Captain de Tracey expressing her desire that the funeral should be at Manby, coupled with a formal invitation to Gwladys to be present on the occasion. And so a few days after the events just recorded, Gwladys found herself with Elizabeth and Captain de Tracey at the door of the house which poor Reggie had so often and so enthusiastically described to her. Bitter as it was, she was yet glad she had come. At least she would see his room and his things, and everything connected with those three happy years of his life, and which she had so often pictured to herself in sleepless nights or when dreaming of her boy. Elizabeth understood this at once, and by a little contrivance with the good old housekeeper, arranged that Gwladys should have her old room as a girl, which opened into the one formerly occupied by Reggie, so that she should be undisturbed in these bitter-sweet recollections. The servants, who had all loved the boy, felt real sympathy for his gentle widowed mother, and were never weary of repeating to her little traits of his goodness and brave spirit, all very soothing to poor Gwladys' heart. And thus, though the duchess was

Q

cold and stiff, and the long dinner terribly trying, and the funeral service the next day chilling in the extreme to one who was used to a different rite, still Gwladys was the better for her little visit, and consented with something like pleasure to accompany Elizabeth the following day to her home. For Mrs. Wilmot had insisted on her deferring her return to her till all these duties were accomplished, with the unselfish and unexpressed hope that perhaps out of all this misery some permanent good might arise with regard to Gwladys' future position and prospects. Loaded by Lady Elizabeth with Reggie's most valuable treasures, including the little Skye-terrier before named, Gwladys the next morning took leave of the duchess; and after one more visit to the still open vault, which contained what was most dear to her on earth, and one more passionate kiss to the pillow of the little bed on which his dear boyish head had so often laid, Gwladys, with tolerable calmness, found herself once more by Lady Elizabeth's side, driving rapidly towards the old-fashioned abbey which was her sister-in-law's present home.

CHAPTER VII.

> So tired, so tired my heart and I!
> Though now none takes me on his arm
> To fold me close and kiss me warm,
> Till each quick breath end in a sigh
> Of happy languor. Now alone—
> . . . .
> 'Tis now we're tired, my heart and I!

THIRLWALL ABBEY, the home to which Elizabeth had brought her sorrowful sister-in-law, had been for upwards of seven hundred years a Benedictine convent, a favourite resort of the Saxon princesses in the good old days, and honoured by the visits of some of England's most famous saints and heroes. Then evil times came of self-indulgence and luxury; and a laxity crept into the religious houses which ruined their spirit, and caused them to fall into disesteem among the people: so that when ambition, avarice, and sensual passion combined to turn the heart of King Henry

VIII. against the Church, he found no great opposition to his scheme for despoiling the fair abbeys, whose riches and lands he coveted, and distributing them among his nobles as a cheap way to himself of defraying their services. And so by *le droit du plus fort* (a doctrine now in universal acceptation, when the wolf everywhere wishes to drink of the lamb's stream), the monks and nuns were turned out on the wide world, and their houses and property seized by the State, which, though bestowing them freely right and left on their vassals, still reserved certain rights and enacted certain acknowledgments of the gift to all time, so as to insure the perpetuity of the robbery, and preclude the possibility of such possessions being ever restored to the Church.

Among the convents so despoiled, Thirlwall was one of the finest. It had been conferred on the Earls of Hoxton, of a noble and illustrious Welsh race, and whose politics and religion had ever been on the side of 'Church and State,' after the fashion still better known in the Elizabethan period. Their names were not found, therefore, in any proscribed roll of the unfortunate royalists in the succeeding century. Rather were they the gaolers than the defenders of the ill-fated Stuart king. Neither did they risk money and blood on behalf of the so-called 'Pretenders' of that luckless house. But they lived on, from father to son, in quiet and continual enjoyment of their beautiful home, adding yearly broader lands to their already large possessions, and altering the abbey from time to time, according to the taste of each succeeding generation.

Thus Inigo Jones had been commissioned to add a south front to Henry VII.th's tower and east wing which Holbein had left, and the result was a magnificent suite of rooms, of perfect proportions, painted and decorated in the purest style of Italian art, and hung with the *chefs-d'œuvre* of Vandyke and other ancient masters.

Another earl had imbibed, in foreign travel, a taste for sculpture and antiquities, and so enriched his gallery with countless treasures of Greece and Rome. Each age had thus done its part towards beautifying and adorning this venerable dwelling, which yet still bore the stamp of its ancient religious foundation.

For the double cloisters remained, running round the four sides of the old quadrangle, in the centre of which stood an early Christian well, its panels beautifully and richly carved with the emblems of the Cross and the Vine, and its open mouth deeply indented by the marks of the rope, which had worn furrows into its marble rim.

These cloisters, glazed in these degenerate days of luxury, were entered from a hall, cockney Gothicised by the relentless Wyatt (Is he in Hades, tormented by perpetual nightmares of the houses his bad taste has ruined?), but rich with armorial suits, taken in one of the famous French battles of old days by the Lord Hoxton of the period, a burly, short, thickset man, whose effigy was placed among that of his prisoners, accoutred in a gorgeous suit of armour engraved with gold. These historical treasures had been concealed during the civil wars in the roof of an adjoining chapelry, from whence they had been rescued by their present possessors. The 'Nun's Walk' still remained, and bore its old name among the peasants. It was a shady yew-covered path, impervious alike to summer's sun or winter's snow.

A small oak-wainscoted room above one which still retained the name of the 'Abbess's parlour,' was said to be the guest-chamber of Cardinal Wolsey during his not unfrequent visits to the abbey. From time to time, when changes had been made in the gardens and grounds, various articles of church furniture would be found: one day, a lamp, an Anglo-Saxon 'gabbatha,' such as were used to burn day and night before the tabernacle: another, a gold ring, evidently worn by the abbess, on which was deeply and clearly cut the inscription: 'Benedicta sit Sta Trinitas.' The convent church had been destroyed, but, on the site of a portion of it, a little oratory had been built for family prayers.

Neither was a ghost-story wanting to add

to the respectability of the place. Night after night, a step was heard, deliberately pacing round and round the cloistered walls; and many a time in bright moonlight, the master of the house or his guests would look out and strive to discover the cause of the unusual sound. But none could ever be found. The legend ran, that it was the restless spirit of that Earl of Hoxton who, when the convent had been given back to the nuns in Queen Mary's time, had, when Queen Elizabeth came to the throne, forcibly repossessed himself of both house and lands, and ejected anew the poor persecuted ladies, with scarcely any previous notice. Less credulous people, however, comforted themselves by attributing the footsteps to some hitherto unascertained but natural causes, quoting the speech of an old gamekeeper on the estate, who, when questioned as to 'whether he did not fear the ghost?' replied: 'No, I don't believe in 'um, for if he were up there (pointing to the sky), he wouldn't want to come down; and if he were down below, they wouldn't let 'um out!'

A beautiful Italian garden had been made on the west side of the house, with a fountain in the centre; and a fine trout stream ran through the lawn in front of the windows, dividing the garden from the park. But the glory of Thirlwall was its cedars, brought from the Lebanon, and worthy of their sires; and under the shade of which, stretched on oriental carpets, the whole family would often spend the summer afternoons; while the great extent of closely-mown and beautifully-kept lawn (that continual marvel to foreigners), and the cool sound of the flowing water under the arches of the bridge (itself a master-work of Palladio), made the spot at that season of the year one of the most perfect luxury and enjoyment that can be conceived. And Lord Hoxton was worthy of this beautiful home. A good landlord, a kind master, courteous and hospitable to his guests, charitable and tolerant both by nature and upon principle, he might be called one of the best specimens of a thoroughly high-bred English country gentleman. His delight was to open his house and grounds on every possible occasion to the neighbourhood, but especially to the poor. He rejoiced in seeing them sitting with their little children grouped under the trees, or watching from the bridge the fat trout as they lazily lay against the piers with their noses up stream; or else playing cricket on a ground he had had carefully enclosed and levelled for the purpose in the park, or dancing on the lawn to the music of the local band, which he greatly encouraged as a means of amusing the young men in their leisure hours. He used to say, with the simplicity which was habitual to him, 'that the only good of having a big place was to be able to give pleasure to so many people.' And they looked upon the grounds and everything belonging to them as sacred, and, as it were, something of their own, something of which they themselves had to be proud of and care for; so that not a flower was touched, nor a branch of a tree broken, even when hundreds had wandered about, through a whole long day, on its velvety lawns. Thus trust begat trust, as it always will; and the link between the employer and the employed grew daily closer and closer. His labourers and servants all loved him: to care for their interests as if they were his own; to give them good and comfortable cottages, with innocent ways of recreation; to educate and help on their children in life; to see after them personally when sick or in trouble; and to be impartially just to all; this it was which made him so greatly beloved.

They had been there all their lives—from the grey-haired house-steward and housekeeper down to the old porter at the lodge and the old housemaid, whose pride was to speak of the days when she got ready 'the best rooms' for the young fair bride who had been Lord Hoxton's mother, and who came there on a visit 'before she was My Lady.' Each and all had identified themselves with the sorrows and joys of 'the family,' as if they alone existed for them in all the world. There was in the churchyard a kind of 'servants' corner,' bright with crosses and gay flowers, where, one by one, these faithful friends were laid. Some after thirty, some after forty, one even after sixty-one years of service; and their master had cheered their dying beds with his presence and kind and soothing words, and had himself accompanied their remains as chief mourner to their last resting-place. And now he had brought home to them a young wife, like-minded, who very soon won her share of their love, although the old porter would sometimes grumble at her ladyship's charities, which he considered too indiscriminate, and declare that 'his life wasn't worth having on soup days!'

Lord Hoxton had another characteristic of an English country gentleman; he was a first-rate sportsman, a capital rider across country, and an excellent shot. But he did not either despise literary or artistic acquirements. His house was the resort of all the cleverest and most remarkable men of the day, and he had the rare quality of making everybody feel *at home* at once. So that people looked on a visit to Thirlwall Abbey as one of the pleasantest episodes of the year, to be marked with a red letter, and repeated as often as their host's hospitality, or their own avocations, would permit. At the same time, he discouraged all 'fast' or fine and scandal-loving society, which had no charms for him or for his gentle loving wife. After all, it was difficult to be bored at Thirlwall, where there was occupation and interest for every taste; pictures and books full of original sketches of the first masters for one; scarce books and first editions for another; billiards for a third; the last new novel or pamphlet for a fourth. Even a wet day gave no excuse for feeling dull! and the charm to visitors was that they were *left alone*, not compelled to 'do this' or to 'see that' to suit the taste of their host or hostess; but allowed to follow their own devices, and do what each liked best. Out of doors, there were plenty of carriages and horses, ponies for timid riders, and basket-carriages for bad walkers, and fishing rods and guns and every other accessory of a *bien monté* country house. That *vie de château*, so little understood out of England (except perhaps in Hungary), and which is the pride of our country, was certainly enjoyed in perfection at Thirlwall; while the brilliant ‚conversation of their host added a fresh charm to the hours of general gathering.

Out of sympathy and feeling for Gwladys, the merry shooting party of the week before had been broken up, and no one remained at Thirlwall but two or three old friends, *habitués* of the house. One, a clever writer, deep in collecting facts in the well-stored library for a forthcoming work; another a celebrated artist, glad to exchange his brush and studio for a few weeks for a fishing-rod and landing-net; and the third, a man of foreign birth and name, but a naturalised Englishman, who had travelled all over the world, and who combined all that was most agreeable and amusing in knowledge and conversation with the kindest and tenderest of hearts. He was indeed a friend in need to rich and poor; deterred by neither distance nor difficulty when a kind action could be done or suffering in any form relieved. Whether it were for the peer, in whose house he was ever a welcome guest, or the starving Irishman dying in the fever which the previous famine had engendered, or the young girl left friendless and destitute, and exposed to every temptation in the London streets—each and all turned to him instinctively in their hour of need, sure of some kind of help from his ever-ready will.

He had heard a great deal of Gwladys both from the Hoxtons and Captain de Tracey, and was very anxious to see and know her.

But Gwladys, on her first arrival, was too much exhausted by all she had gone through, to do more than go to her own room; and the next morning to lie still in Elizabeth's boudoir (the abbess's parlour before named), where she breakfasted quietly, and then sat in the deep window seat, gazing listlessly on the beautiful view before her, and striving to stop the tears which would well up from her full heart as she thought of Reggie.

Elizabeth brought her some hot-house

flowers, and asked her to arrange them in a basket on the table, which she knew was in general a great pleasure to her. But the flowers only brought back to her her old home, and with it recollections of even a sadder sort. For the reaction which Captain de Tracey had feared for Gwladys after the intense excitement of the preceding ten days, had produced a depression and a hopeless despondency in her mind which affected likewise her bodily health. A kind of low fever came on every night, depriving her of all sleep till morning; and then would come the weary feeling of 'What use was there in getting up?—there was no one who would care if she did or not.'

She had arrived at that stage of utter indifference to all that befell her, when she was roused by a letter from Father St. Clair, in answer to one written by her, giving the account of Reggie's illness and death. It ran as follows:—

'My dear Lady William,—Your letter filled me with intense sorrow and sympathy, and yet with untold consolation. Surely you may indeed rejoice in the midst of your natural anguish, that he should have been taken at that age, in his purity and innocence; that he should have died, though ignorant of Catholic truth, in such perfect dispositions of contrition, faith, and love; and that you should have been permitted to watch over him to the last, with the assurance that he is now among the angels of God. What more can a Christian mother ask for her child? Still, you must not fancy for a moment that I do not enter into your human sorrow, and feel for you with my whole heart. I know that the very qualities which made him fit for the Great Reaper endeared him to you more and more, and that all life must henceforth wear to you a sad and colourless aspect. But I want you to think of how much more bitter it would have been for you to have seen him grow up like most young men of his class now-a-days —wild, self-indulgent, careless of God and of holy things, having learned to despise and vilify his mother's faith, and contemning all guidance or authority in matters of religion?

Surely, a sharper sword would then have pierced through your mother's heart than that which has wounded it now. For sickness and death come direct from God's hand—not like sin, which comes from ourselves; and therefore all the sorrow that fills your poor heart is from Him who loves you with a love passing human knowledge, and who has meted out to you just that proportion of suffering which He knows to be best for you, to lead you, by His own paths, towards your true home. There is no such school as that of sorrow, the one in which He lived all His life, and of which He and His· mother are the guides and comforters. But I will say no more now; you have your crucifix with you, and that is your Master. Study those wounds. St. Jerome compares them to mines of gold, and tells us how we must work them, by digging deep and throwing away, as the miner does, the superfluous earth and stones and rubble; that is, in casting aside all that is earthly in our affections, and laying hold of the rich ore of consolation ever flowing from those fountains of priceless blood. And now, may God bless and comfort you, dear child, as He alone can. Let me know if there is anything I can do for you at any time, and treat me always with all confidence, and without apologies or excuses for anything you may say to me, or may want of me.

'Your faithful friend and
'Servant in Jesus Christ,
'FRANCIS ST. CLAIR.'

The wonderful effect in cheering and strengthening Gwladys' heart which this letter produced suggested to Lady Elizabeth a little surprise for her, which she communicated to her husband, who gladly came in to her proposal; and the result was that a few evenings after, as Gwladys was lying down on a sofa by a bright wood fire, which the approach of autumn rendered very acceptable to an invalid, the door opened, and Father St. Clair was announced. The joy of seeing him again, and of having some one with whom she could speak freely of the things nearest her heart, was almost more than Gwladys' strength could bear, for in spite of all her sister-in-law's kindness, there was between them that most insuperable though intangible of all barriers, the difference of faith, which precluded all thorough confidence or sympathy between them, and insensibly 'tabooed' a score of subjects as touching on dangerous ground, which were nevertheless the only ones of real interest to Gwladys herself. And Father St. Clair was a man eminently qualified to comfort and cheer all those with whom he came in contact. The eldest son of an old Catholic family, brought up for the army, and with all the qualities and personal attractions which would have ensured his success in the world, he had suddenly resolved to abandon all, to sacrifice all, and to bear all, for the sake of Him who had filled him with this earnest love and devotion to His service. Crushing as with an iron hand his natural tastes, his exuberant human affections, even in their most legitimate form, he entered bravely on the hard and narrow way of poverty, self-denial, mortification and renouncement of all earthly or personal joys. And the result was a spirit entirely detached from all that did not concern God's glory, a thirst for souls which made him regard all danger, fatigue, and pain as nothing if thereby he could win more soldiers for Christ.

Gwladys was rejoiced that her Protestant relations should be thrown in close personal intercourse with such a specimen of a Catholic priest, while his cleverness, fun, and great literary acquirements (which his knowledge of most modern languages placed far above the average) made him a most agreeable companion to Lord Hoxton and to Captain de Tracey, whose prejudices against his 'cloth' were dispelled by actual contact with a man of his sort, in a way which years of argument would have failed to effect.

During his visit, Gwladys had one or two earnest conversations with him as to her future life. There was no object left for her remaining in England, of which the climate was telling seriously on her health and constitution; and so, by his advice, she wrote a long letter to Mrs. Vere, detailing the events of the last three years, and proposing to come to her if she wished, and endeavour as far as possible to fulfil a child's love and duty towards her. In the meantime, she decided to return to Mrs. Wilmot's, and there wait patiently for the answer, which could not be received for two or three months. Strangely enough, in spite of her freedom from all human ties, and her strong sense of religion and love of the poor, she felt no vocation for a religious life. She dreaded its monotony, doubted her own stability and strength to live a life so entirely above human affections. And Father St. Clair never attempted to turn her thoughts in that direction, feeling equally convinced that this was not the line which God in His providence had marked out for her.

'And supposing Mrs. Vere should be gone or dead, and this plan fail,' said Gwladys, one day at the end of a long talk on these subjects, 'what shall I do then?'

'Do not foresee or forecast, my child;

simply *trust*,' replied Father St. Clair, gravely. 'You are ever inclined, not unnaturally, perhaps, to look on the darker side; and it is not always the true one. God is jealous of our managements and plans. He likes us to abandon ourselves entirely to Him, and He will order all things for our greater good. Will you try and believe this? I have a conviction that better days are in store for you,' he added, more cheerily, 'and that the cloudy and stormy morning of your life will end in perhaps a glowing sunset!'— words which filled Gwladys' heart with more strength and brightness than she could have believed possible a week before.

And now, feeling that she had no longer any excuse for delaying a return to her duties at Mrs. Wilmot's, and not wishing to abuse her great and considerate kindness, she wrote to announce her return, asking likewise permission to bring her boy's little dog, which had become so greatly endeared to her by its loving winsome ways, that she felt she could scarcely bear to have him out of her sight. He had attached himself to her as dogs do, in a marvellous way, to those who have loved their former masters; and when the tears rained down her cheeks, as they still would do at times, when little inanimate things reminded her of her heavy loss, he would scramble up into her lap and lick them off her face, and endeavour, by every little artifice in his power, to cheer and comfort her.

'I own I often think there is nothing so real and so true as *dog love*,' exclaimed Elizabeth one day, after watching Eric's determined and continued efforts to win a smile and a kiss from his sad mistress. 'Here have I been trying to tempt him out with me this quarter of an hour; but no, he won't leave your sofa, Gwladys; he goes a little way and then hangs his head and trots back, just as if he had said to himself: "No, I must wait till she's stronger, and can go too."'

Gwladys laughed and patted his grey head, on which Eric gave a whine of delight, and proceeded to scamper wildly about the room.

'You and I must go out for a walk to-morrow,' she said cheerfully, looking at the dog. 'And now what am I to say to you, you tenderest of sisters, for all the patience and love you have showered upon me, and the way you have borne with my sad ungrateful humours,' continued Gwladys, gently drawing down Elizabeth's face to hers and warmly kissing her. 'I am afraid I must say, like the poor people, "I can do nothing but pray for you."'

'And do you think I reckon that nothing?' gaily replied Elizabeth. 'On the contrary, I begin to believe you are right and all of us wrong,' she added more gravely; 'anyhow, you and Father St. Clair seem to have learned a secret of peace and acquiescence in God's will which I, for one, have not attained.'

Captain de Tracey's entrance at that moment interrupted their conversation.

'Is it true, really true, that she is going back next week, Elizabeth?' he exclaimed in an injured tone; 'just as she was getting better, and we had planned lots of expeditions with her. Why must you go back to that old woman,' he continued, turning to Gwladys, 'instead of stopping here with your natural relations and getting quite strong and well?'

'He that will not work neither let him eat,' replied Gwladys, laughing. 'There's a proverb for you as old as Adam. You know I must earn my bread like a sensible woman, and not get demoralised by such a *dolce far niente* life as I have been leading here, spoiled and petted by everybody all round.' But Captain de Tracey seemed pained at her light tone, and kept flicking his riding-whip impatiently on his boots to conceal his irritation; and Elizabeth being summoned at this moment out of the room, he and Gwladys were left alone. For the first time a sense of extreme awkwardness at their mutual position came over her, and a sort of instinct of what was coming, but before she could escape to her own room he had spoken:

'Lady William—Gwladys—it's no use my holding my tongue any longer. I can't have you go away and earn your bread, as you call it, among strangers. I have cared for you ever since I saw you that first evening in those poor little lodgings! and every day I have struggled in vain against the feeling, fearing that I should never be good enough for you, and that you would never like such a one as I am. But I love you with all my heart and soul, and I would do anything to become what you wish, if you will only give me some hope, some little hope,' he added imploringly, looking up under her cast-down eyes, as if striving to read his fate there.

Gwladys was pained beyond words at this unexpected declaration, but she never hesitated in her answer.

'It is impossible. Oh! do not speak of such things,' she exclaimed in a piteous tone of distress. 'Let me look upon you as a brother, as a "real cousin," as you said to me that first day; but do not grieve me by asking for that which I cannot give—which I have given away already,' she murmured in a lower tone, but which was not lost on Captain de Tracey, who started as if he had been stung.

'Whom could you have seen? Who

has forestalled me?' he exclaimed, almost fiercely.

'Listen to me,' replied Gwladys gravely 'while I tell you something of my previous history; and then you will see how impossible it is for me to listen to your words.'

He sat down mechanically where she bid him; and then, in a few simple words, she told him of her early, though blighted, love; of her pledge to Walter; of her forced and miserable marriage; and of her invincible resolution to remain faithful to that which had been her first and only love. She spoke quietly and calmly, but with a decision which Captain de Tracey felt it would be hopeless to combat. He rose when she had finished, and said sadly and sorrowfully:

'Gwladys, forgive me; I did not know all this; and forget what I said just now; let it make no difference in our mutual intercourse. It would break my heart if you were to cease to treat me as an old friend.'

Gwladys gladly promised, and warmly pressing his hand, took refuge in her own room. She felt, however, that it was impossible for her presence at that moment to be otherwise than painful to him; and so it was a relief to her, on coming in, to find a letter on her table which had come by the cross-post from Mrs. Wilmot, in answer to her proposal of a speedy return.

'My dear Lady William,' she wrote, 'I am delighted at the thought of having you back, for though Carter is very attentive to me, she cannot supply your place; and I specially miss our French readings together. By all means, bring the little dog. I shall rejoice at anything which may make my dull home brighter to you. If you could come on Tuesday—sleeping Monday night in London— my servant is coming down by the morning express on that day, and would take care of you and your boxes. I will tell him to look out for you. Your affectionate,

'M. C. WILMOT.'

This was Friday, and Gwladys felt that it would be better for her, if she could, to accompany Father St. Clair the following morning, who was returning to London for his Sunday duty, and spend a couple of days in a convent, where she had already been on several previous occasions, and where she was sure of a hearty welcome from both the mother and the community. The obvious advantage of an escort on both journeys would, she knew, blind the eyes of her kind hosts to her real motive, and Captain de Tracey would, in his heart, feel grateful to her for thus relieving his embarrassment. So she took an opportunity of speaking quietly to Father St. Clair before dinner, who had his own private suspicions as to the state of the case, though he said nothing to Gwladys; and so, when she announced her intention of taking leave of them all the following day, a few quiet words from him made the whole thing appear natural, and as a matter of course, and Gwladys was spared the pain of a long argument in favour of her remaining longer, which she would otherwise have found it rather difficult to evade.

Taking leave the following morning of all these loving hearts, not without some natural sorrow, and the feeling that it was as if another link were broken which bound her to her boy, the train conveyed her quickly to King's Cross, where, wishing good-bye to Father St. Clair, she proceeded to her quiet convent home. It was an untold relief to her to find herself once more in that little blue chapel, kneeling before the Blessed Sacrament, and to be able to pour out all her sorrows into the tender sympathising ear of the loving mother superior, who cared for her as for a sister, and with whom she was happier than with any one else in England. The night prayers, the early repetition in choir of the divine office, the solemn and beautiful communion which followed, to which several young girls (dressed in pure white muslin) were for the first time admitted, all acted as a soothing balm to Gwladys' sore heart, and restored her failing faith and courage, so that it was with a brave spirit, though with a tear in her eye, that she took leave on the Tuesday morning of that loving community, and went forth once more into the crowded world of London alone.

CHAPTER VIII.

L'amour n'a qu'un mot.
                    LACORDAIRE.

THE following winter was spent at Torquay, in a succession of daily duties and simple pleasures which left Gwladys little time for morbid thought. Still there were hours when her sorrow would press heavily upon her, and moments also when she became anxious for an answer from the Mauritius. One day, when she had been toiling rather wearily and despondingly up the steep hill which leads to the villas on the warmer side of that picturesque watering-place, a gentleman stopped her, and asked her if she could kindly tell him the address of a Mrs. Wilmot, who, he had been told, was living in one of the houses near. Gwladys told him she was going there herself, and in a few moments the door was reached.

'May I ask your name, sir?' said Gwladys, before ushering him into Mrs. Wilmot's room.

'My name is McCarthy, Captain McCarthy,' he continued; 'but my business is not, strictly speaking, with her, but with a Lady William de Tracey, who is, I believe, living with her at this moment.'

'Pray come in, sir,' replied Gwladys, 'I am the person you seek. We shall be able to talk more comfortably in the drawing-room.'

She opened the door, and introducing the stranger to Mrs. Wilmot, sat down and waited for him to speak. But Captain McCarthy seemed strangely embarrassed; and Mrs. Wilmot, wishing to put him at his ease, began talking to him of the beauty of Torquay, its walks and climate, in which, however, it was evident the stranger took little interest. At last, summoning up all his courage, Captain McCarthy addressed himself to Gwladys.

'I have just arrived from India,' he said, rather abruptly, with a marked emphasis on the word, at which he saw her visibly colour, while her hands clasped themselves more tightly together. 'I have a great friend there,' he continued; 'one of the best and noblest fellows that ever lived; and when I got leave to come home, he charged me to leave no stone unturned to find you out, and to deliver into your own hands this packet'— giving her a large parcel of letters as he spoke; and then, taking pity on her evident emotion at his unexpected words, he turned to Mrs. Wilmot, and began an ordinary 'wind and weather' conversation on the topics of the day. Gwladys was grateful to him for his delicacy and consideration, and yet burning to ask him some further questions, while not daring to open the letters until she could find herself alone and undisturbed. Captain McCarthy adroitly led Mrs. Wilmot to talk of his arrival in England, and then said, addressing himself to both ladies at once:

'Yes, I have got six months' holiday, and came home overland, leaving my old friend Colonel Vere very enviously watching me on the pier, as we steamed out of the mouth of the Ganges. But he was on the point of starting for the Nilgherries, the healthiest station in the world, you know, where his regiment is now quartered for the summer months. If you will allow me,' he continued, turning specially to Gwladys, ' I will call again to-morrow, when you have had time to read your letters, and see whether you have any answer to give me;' and so saying, he bowed and left them.

It required all the patience and self-control which Gwladys had learned in the school of trial, to answer quietly Mrs. Wilmot's inquiries as to 'who Colonel Vere was?' and ' whether she had known him in the Mauritius?' and the like questions, which very naturally followed from Captain McCarthy's unexpected visit; and still more trying were the succeeding hours of dinner and tea, and subsequent reading out loud, when poor Gwladys in vain endeavoured to fix her attention on the fate of the hero and heroine who were the subjects of the tale. At last night came, and with it an unusual sleepiness in good old Mrs. Wilmot, who, to Gwladys' great joy, suggested an earlier move to bed than usual.

> Although the day be never so long,
> At length it ringeth to evensong!

So runs the old ballad, and so thought Gwladys when, her duties fulfilled, and Mrs. Wilmot comfortably tucked up for the night, she was at last free to go to her own room, and locking her door, busy herself in the perusal of the precious letters which had all day long burned in her pocket. The sight of the well-known, clear, bold handwriting, so dearly loved, and which for years she had never dared trust herself to look at, or to think of, overcame her to such a degree that she could only at first see through her blinding tears without being able to take in the sense of a single word. By degrees she became calmer and began to read, and as she read, an expression of such joy and such love lit up her features that no one who had seen her only in England would have recognised the 'sad widow lady' whose smile even would sometimes make people cry. And when she had finished the letter, she threw herself on her knees by her little bed and cried out loud, 'O! my God, I thank Thee; forgive my faithlessness and fears. I thank and bless Thee now and for evermore!'

Yes, Father St. Clair was right. 'Brighter days were in store for her,' and brighter days had come indeed. Repentance and suffering patiently borne had, in God's mercy, blotted out the faults of her early life, and months of misery were to give place to years of pure and holy joy.

Colonel Vere wrote as follows:—

'Gwladys, my own Gwladys, I may call thee so once more, may I not? After all these cruel years of misery, separation, and wrong, I once more write to claim thee as my own. I know all thy life since that terrible day (which even now I shudder to think of) which saw thee forcibly dragged from thy home, and sent with that man across that cruel sea. I followed thee in heart through all thy Australian trials. I felt (God forgive me!) a joy unspeakable when

Colonel Vere's Letter.   263

that man died and thou wert free. And I understood well that delicate shrinking from coming back to thine old home, and then the sense of duty and self-sacrifice (that was *my* Gwladys all the world over!) which took thee to England for thy boy. And I know all those people's cruelty towards thee there, and how bravely thou didst bear it all for his sake. And now I know how the end is come, and how thy poor mother's heart has been riven, and how thou art now alone. Come, Gwladys, come, my own darling life (Dost thou recollect my old pet name for thee?); come, and let that heart be healed and soothed by my ever-faithful love. I may not leave my post here. I may not come and fetch thee, as my poor beating heart so longs to do! But thou canst come to me; thou canst *trust* me, canst thou not, after all these weary years of hopeless love and waiting? O! my own, I kneel down at thy feet and look up with streaming eyes in thy dear face, and say, O! come to me; come and let me atone to thee by years of loving tenderness for all that thou hast suffered since thou wert torn from me. I have written to my darling mother. She, too, echoes my prayer to thee. The bearer of this letter is my dearest friend; he will arrange everything for thy voyage, for I have told him all my hopes and fears. I would give all the world to see thee opening this, for I know how lovingly thy dear brown eyes would look, eyes that I have dreamed of and cried for night after night, sobbing on my pillow, O! so heart-breakingly. But all that is past now. I have ever loved thee, and cared for thee, and prayed for thee, and trusted thee with all my heart, and soul, and strength, and as none other could, and for ever and ever and evermore, I am thine own faithful Walter.

'P.S. Come, come, come! and O! come quickly!'

Another letter was enclosed, giving all the necessary details as to voyage and outfit, and adding a cheque to defray both. He had arranged everything with a minute thoughtfulness which only love could teach. A letter from Mrs. Vere followed close on the heels of her son's, and was an answer to Gwladys' proposal. She wrote:—

'My darling Child,—Your touching letter has just been brought to me, but tempting as the proposal is, I must not accept it. There is one who has a greater right to you than I. Make him happy, my Gwladys, and I shall wish for no other proof of your filial love. When you are once married, I shall have nothing left to do on earth but to sing the 'Nunc Dimittis,' and thank God.

'Your devoted mother,

'E. Vere.'

No sleep visited Gwladys' eyes that night. She was too happy, too excited, too thankful to do ought but pray and thank God for this unspeakable mercy. She had almost forgotten what happiness was like in those weary fifteen years of continual anxiety or sorrow. But now it came back to her as with a flood. 'Heaviness may endure for a night, but joy cometh in the morning.' She seemed to realise these words in a way she had never before dreamed of. The early dawn found her in the little church on the hill, offering her joyful mass of thanksgiving, and then she hurried home and poured into Mrs. Wilmot's astonished ears her whole tale of past sorrow and of coming happiness. And the old lady cried and laughed by turns, and kissed Gwladys again and again, and in her unselfish joy tried to shut out the sad thoughts which would arise when she felt how terribly she would miss that gentle loving presence, and what a blank her own future life would be without her. And before the morning was over Captain McCarthy had come back, and Gwladys, sitting by his side, was listening with glistening eyes to all he had to tell her of Walter and of the honours he had won, and of all the events great and small which had happened to him during his Indian career; and Captain McCarthy, as he looked at her, no longer wondered at his friend's devotion, and only rejoiced in his heart at having had any share, however small, in bringing about the reunion of two such faithful hearts. It was finally arranged that she should start for Calcutta the following month, where Colonel Vere would meet her; and Captain McCarthy undertook to introduce her to some old friends of his who were returning to India by that mail, and would serve as an escort during her voyage and as chaperones on the still more delicate and nervous occasion of her first arrival at Calcutta to meet her betrothed.

'Mrs. Marley is a thorough lady, a true woman, and a good Catholic besides,' said Captain McCarthy, when discussing this portion of the subject. 'You could not be in better or safer hands, for she is a real friend in need. And I know she will be only too delighted to be of some little service to you, and still more when she comes to know you,' he added, smiling at Gwladys, whom this arrangement relieved from the only lurking fear she had of her proceeding being looked upon as rather a forward one by some ill-natured people who did not know all the circumstances of the case.

So an answer was despatched to Walter

from them both. We need not doubt the tenour of either. And letters were likewise written by Gwladys to Lady Elizabeth and Father St. Clair, and last, not least, to poor Captain de Tracey, to whom she felt this mark of confidence was due for his past unvarying kindness towards her. His answer was characteristic, and accompanied with the most beautiful travelling bag which Asprey could produce.

'My dear Cousin Gwladys,—I wish you joy with all my heart, and think Colonel Vere the luckiest dog upon earth; but I feel I don't deserve such happiness myself. I hope you will let me know him when you come back to England, and that you wont forget your promise to pray for a poor devil like me, whose only chance of going to the right place is by being helped by people of your sort. God bless you, and give you a safe voyage.

'S. DE TRACEY.'

One only visit Gwladys resolved to pay before leaving England, and that was to the grave of her boy. The duchess was in London, and there was no one but the old porter to receive her when she rang once more at the fine old gateway, and was admitted by the kind-hearted housekeeper into that house so full to her of sad and bitter memories. The good old woman hurried to have her room prepared and to get her some tea, whilst Gwladys walked quickly down the well-known corridor of the passage to the corner where Reggie's rocking-horse still remained untouched, and to the little cupboard where he kept his boat and his carpenter's tools, and so on to his own little room, Eric preceding her, and every now and then giving a low whine of recognition as he smelt some well-known object in his old haunts, and yet missed the little master who had always been his playmate there. Gwladys opened the shutter, which in the empty state of the house had been left closed, and the pale rays of the wintry sun fell on Reggie's little hunting-whip and fox's brush, which, with boyish taste, he had hung as a trophy above his bed, and on the book of MS. prayers written and illuminated for him by her as a parting gift when the bitter hour of their first separation came. Spite of all her new-found and newly-restored happiness, Gwladys could not yet bear unmoved the sight of all these things so dear to her mother's heart, and the housekeeper on coming to fetch her found her sobbing on the little bed as if her loss were but of yesterday.

'There, there, my lady, don't take on so—now pray, don't,' exclaimed the kind old woman in much distress. 'I know it's very hard to bear; I lost a son myself once,' and at the words her voice faltered; 'but he was not so young and innocent as Master Reggie. God bless him! You have everything to comfort you, my lady, in thinking of him.'

'Yes, I know, I know,' murmured poor Gwladys, striving to recover her self-control; 'but it was the sight of all his things, and —'

'And very natural too, my lady, I'm sure; only now do come down and have a hot cup of tea; it's all ready for you in the blue drawing-room, and you must be pretty nearly schrammed up in this cold room all this time;' and so saying, Gwladys was coaxed and led downstairs by the good woman, who had the satisfaction of seeing her really enjoy the meal which her thoughtful kindness had prepared for her. After a few minutes she left the room, and then returning with a key in her hand, said with some hesitation:

'I thought you would wish for this, my lady. It's all very nice and dry, only there are no flowers on the path now as there are in summer time.'

Gwladys pressed her kind hand in silent thanks, and taking the key, went out of the library door, and through the garden to the quiet churchyard, and to the crypt where her darling's little coffin was laid. Long did she stay and pray there for the soul so dear to her, and then with a sob in her heart at the thought of the many years it might be before she should again kneel by that flat cross which distinguished her boy's earthly resting-place from the gorgeous coroneted coffins beside him, she softly closed the iron door, and retraced her steps to the house. It was too late to think of returning to town that evening, so she gladly accepted the offered bed, and was soothed by the garrulity of the old housekeeper, who had so loved her child, and who was never weary of the topic ever present to Gwladys' mind. Taking leave of her the next day, and rejoicing her by the gift of a brooch with Reggie's photograph on one side, and a lock of his bright curling hair on the other, Gwladys went back to London, where the necessary preparations for her long voyage absorbed all the time she could spare from Lady Elizabeth, who had come up to town on purpose to see her off, and who was ingenious in thinking of and providing every imaginable article for her comfort on the way. And so the last morning came, and a little knot of people were grouped on the platform of the London Bridge station in the dusky light of a February morning. Captain McCarthy was there to introduce her to Colonel and Mrs. Marley, who lost their hearts to Gwladys at once, as he had foretold; and Father St. Clair, who had said his mass an hour earlier that she might share in it; and Lady Elizabeth and Captain de Tracey with a preservative from sea-sickness, and a tiny bottle of champagne for the like object, which he insisted on thrusting into her already over-full bag at the last moment. And then the signal was given, the guard's shrill whistle sounded, and the Dover express glided rapidly out of the station-house, leaving a somewhat sad little group behind.

'Well, God bless her on land and sea,' murmured Captain de Tracey as he drew Elizabeth's arm within his and walked back to her carriage. 'She has had sorrow enough in England, God knows, to make her glad enough to leave the country.'

'But she leaves plenty of pleasant memories behind her, and a bright example too,' replied Father St. Clair. 'I never met with one whose whole life was such an example of self-sacrifice. Whenever I felt inclined to flag, the thoughts of her would brace me up and make me ashamed of my cowardice. Ah! Lady Elizabeth,' he continued, as he shook hands with her at the carriage door, 'you women may be called

T

the weaker sex, but you have often braver hearts than we, with all our boasting;' and so saying, he wished good-bye to Gwladys' faithful friends, and jumped into the hansom which was to convey him home.

The journey and voyage to Paris were uneventful. That beautiful capital was new to Gwladys, but she could not stay to see it and run the risk of being too late for the Indian mail. So the following evening saw her once more in the railway, with her good friends the Marleys, Eric remonstrating with all his lungs at the dog-box to which the inexorable guard had condemned him. Thirty-six hours brought them to Marseilles, from whence they were at once transferred to the deck of the 'Massilia,' one of the Peninsular and Oriental Company's fastest boats to Alexandria. How that town and Cairo reminded her of Reginald, and of his childish delight at the first sight of the long files of camels in the streets, it is not necessary to say. Suez was their next resting-place, with its arid shores and hot sands, and mixture of English and Indian inhabitants; and then they found themselves once more in one of those magnificent vessels, where the ever-going 'punkah' deprives the cabin passenger of half the usual suffering on other tropical lines. In proportion as they neared their destination, Gwladys' joy and yet her nervousness increased. For the first time she recollected, with something like a sharp pang of pain, how altered she was in the last fifteen years; how sorrow had given lines to her brow and faded her cheek, and was beginning even to silver her hair here and there. Would he love her as he had done in the pride of her youth and beauty? The thought was unworthy of him, and she felt it was so, and yet it would perpetually recur. She little knew how, if she had lost in one way, she had gained in another; and how the sweetness of divine love and of accepted sorrow had given her an expression far beyond any mere earthly beauty. So, with a mixture of intense longing and yet shrinking fear, she watched from the vessel's deck the ever-nearing harbour. A mail boat came alongside; several gentlemen appeared on the poop. One came forward to where she stood. One look was enough to dispel her fears and all the faithless imaginings of her humility.

Regardless of the lookers-on, Colonel Vere clasped her for an instant in his arms, and then introducing her to his companion, who was in the dress of a clergyman, he whispered to her: 'Everything is ready. You do not mind, do you? It is better so. We will go to the cathedral directly you land.'

Gwladys minded nothing then; her joy and thankfulness were too great for words. Yes, there stood Walter by her side, unchanged save that his skin was bronzed by exposure to the sun, and his curly brown hair was thinned and short; but the face was the same—the same loving eyes and delicate mouth, the same open brow which had known no shame, the same look of trust and perfect love which she had parted with, it seemed but the other day, on the steps of her island home. And he; he scarcely dared look at her as she gently led him up to the Marleys, and he thanked them with all his heart for their kind care of her during their six weeks' acquaintance. And then they sat side by side, almost in silence, except that his eyes would moisten from time to time, and his old cry of 'darling Life' came in a whisper from his lips as he pressed her little hand in his. And so the wharf was reached and the moment of landing came.

Gwladys and her faithful friends went straight as he had wished to the church, where God's blessing was at last to crown this long-deferred and holy union. And all was ready as he said, and the solemn service proceeded. Walter's 'I will' reverberated through the aisles as if he would have had it heard of men and of angels. And the Communion followed and still further sanctified that sacred rite; and Colonel and Mrs. Vere rose with glad and thankful hearts, and thus began together that life of pure love on earth which would be perfected hereafter in the kingdom of God.

www.ingramcontent.com/pod-product-compliance
Lightning Source LLC
Chambersburg PA
CBHW032140230426
43672CB00011B/2403